Web Customer Support
Complete Self-Assessment Guide

C000070055

The guidance in this Self-Assessment is based on Web Customer Support best practices and standards in business process architecture, design and quality management. The guidance is also based on the professional judgment of the individual collaborators listed in the Acknowledgments.

Table of Contents

Included Resources - how to access

Included with your purchase of the book is the Web Customer Support Self-Assessment Spreadsheet Dashboard which contains all questions and Self-Assessment areas and auto-generates insights, graphs, and project RACI planning - all with examples to get you started right away.

How? Simply send an email to
access@theartofservice.com
with this books' title in the subject to get the Web Customer Support Self Assessment Tool right away.

You will receive the following contents with New and Updated specific criteria:

• The latest quick edition of the book in PDF

• The latest complete edition of the book in PDF, which criteria correspond to the criteria in...

• The Self-Assessment Excel Dashboard, and...

• Example pre-filled Self-Assessment Excel Dashboard to get familiar with results generation

• In-depth specific Checklists covering the topic

• Project management checklists and templates to assist with implementation

INCLUDES LIFETIME SELF ASSESSMENT UPDATES

Every self assessment comes with Lifetime Updates and Lifetime Free Updated Books. Lifetime Updates is an industry-first feature which allows you to receive verified self assessment updates, ensuring you always have the most accurate information at your fingertips.

Get it now- you will be glad you did - do it now, before you forget.

Send an email to **access@theartofservice.com** with this books' title in the subject to get the Web Customer Support Self Assessment Tool right away.

Your feedback is invaluable to us

If you recently bought this book, we would love to hear from you! You can do this by writing a review on amazon (or the online store where you purchased this book) about your last purchase! As part of our continual service improvement process, we love to hear real client experiences and feedback.

How does it work?
To post a review on Amazon, just log in to your account and click on the Create Your Own Review button (under Customer Reviews) of the relevant product page. You can find examples of product reviews in Amazon. If you purchased from another online store, simply follow their procedures.

What happens when I submit my review?
Once you have submitted your review, send us an email at review@theartofservice.com with the link to your review so we can properly thank you for your feedback.

Purpose of this Self-Assessment

This Self-Assessment has been developed to improve understanding of the requirements and elements of Web Customer Support, based on best practices and standards in business process architecture, design and quality management.

It is designed to allow for a rapid Self-Assessment to determine how closely existing management practices and procedures correspond to the elements of the Self-Assessment.

The criteria of requirements and elements of Web Customer Support have been rephrased in the format of a Self-Assessment questionnaire, with a seven-criterion scoring system, as explained in this document.

In this format, even with limited background knowledge of

Web Customer Support, a manager can quickly review existing operations to determine how they measure up to the standards. This in turn can serve as the starting point of a 'gap analysis' to identify management tools or system elements that might usefully be implemented in the organization to help improve overall performance.

How to use the Self-Assessment

On the following pages are a series of questions to identify to what extent your Web Customer Support initiative is complete in comparison to the requirements set in standards.

To facilitate answering the questions, there is a space in front of each question to enter a score on a scale of '1' to '5'.

1 Strongly Disagree

2 Disagree

3 Neutral

4 Agree

5 Strongly Agree

Read the question and rate it with the following in front of mind:

**'In my belief,
the answer to this question is clearly defined'.**

There are two ways in which you can choose to interpret this statement;
1. how aware are you that the answer to the question is clearly defined
2. for more in-depth analysis you can choose to gather

evidence and confirm the answer to the question. This obviously will take more time, most Self-Assessment users opt for the first way to interpret the question and dig deeper later on based on the outcome of the overall Self-Assessment.

A score of '1' would mean that the answer is not clear at all, where a '5' would mean the answer is crystal clear and defined. Leave emtpy when the question is not applicable or you don't want to answer it, you can skip it without affecting your score. Write your score in the space provided.

After you have responded to all the appropriate statements in each section, compute your average score for that section, using the formula provided, and round to the nearest tenth. Then transfer to the corresponding spoke in the Web Customer Support Scorecard on the second next page of the Self-Assessment.

Your completed Web Customer Support Scorecard will give you a clear presentation of which Web Customer Support areas need attention.

Web Customer Support Scorecard Example

Example of how the finalized Scorecard can look like:

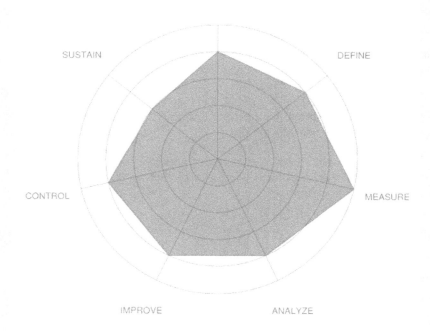

Web Customer Support Scorecard

Your Scores:

BEGINNING OF THE SELF-ASSESSMENT:

CRITERION #1: RECOGNIZE

INTENT: Be aware of the need for change. Recognize that there is an unfavorable variation, problem or symptom.

In my belief, the answer to this question is clearly defined:

5 Strongly Agree

4 Agree

3 Neutral

2 Disagree

1 Strongly Disagree

1. How can auditing be a preventative security measure?
<--- Score

2. When a Web customer support manager recognizes a problem, what options are available?
<--- Score

3. What vendors make products that address the Web

customer support needs?
<--- Score

4. Are losses recognized in a timely manner?
<--- Score

5. How are the Web customer support's objectives aligned to the group's overall stakeholder strategy?
<--- Score

6. Do you have/need 24-hour access to key personnel?
<--- Score

7. Are problem definition and motivation clearly presented?
<--- Score

8. Did you miss any major Web customer support issues?
<--- Score

9. What do employees need in the short term?
<--- Score

10. What are the stakeholder objectives to be achieved with Web customer support?
<--- Score

11. What Web customer support events should you attend?
<--- Score

12. Who are your key stakeholders who need to sign off?
<--- Score

13. What activities does the governance board need to consider?
<--- Score

14. How do you recognize an objection?
<--- Score

15. To what extent does each concerned units management team recognize Web customer support as an effective investment?
<--- Score

16. Will a response program recognize when a crisis occurs and provide some level of response?
<--- Score

17. How much are sponsors, customers, partners, stakeholders involved in Web customer support?
In other words, what are the risks, if Web customer support does not deliver successfully?
<--- Score

18. Can management personnel recognize the monetary benefit of Web customer support?
<--- Score

19. What problems are you facing and how do you consider Web customer support will circumvent those obstacles?
<--- Score

20. Are there Web customer support problems defined?
<--- Score

21. Are employees recognized or rewarded for performance that demonstrates the highest levels of integrity?
<--- Score

22. What are the clients issues and concerns?
<--- Score

23. Does the problem have ethical dimensions?
<--- Score

24. What does Web customer support success mean to the stakeholders?
<--- Score

25. What are your needs in relation to Web customer support skills, labor, equipment, and markets?
<--- Score

26. Are controls defined to recognize and contain problems?
<--- Score

27. What do you need to start doing?
<--- Score

28. Are there regulatory / compliance issues?
<--- Score

29. Are you dealing with any of the same issues today as yesterday? What can you do about this?
<--- Score

30. Who needs to know?
<--- Score

31. What needs to stay?
<--- Score

32. What are the minority interests and what amount of minority interests can be recognized?
<--- Score

33. Are there recognized Web customer support problems?
<--- Score

34. Why is this needed?
<--- Score

35. Do you know what you need to know about Web customer support?
<--- Score

36. What Web customer support capabilities do you need?
<--- Score

37. How do you identify subcontractor relationships?
<--- Score

38. Who defines the rules in relation to any given issue?
<--- Score

39. How do you assess your Web customer support workforce capability and capacity needs, including skills, competencies, and staffing levels?
<--- Score

40. Would you recognize a threat from the inside?
<--- Score

41. Is the quality assurance team identified?
<--- Score

42. How many trainings, in total, are needed?
<--- Score

43. What training and capacity building actions are needed to implement proposed reforms?
<--- Score

44. What is the Web customer support problem definition? What do you need to resolve?
<--- Score

45. Who else hopes to benefit from it?
<--- Score

46. How do you identify the kinds of information that you will need?
<--- Score

47. Whom do you really need or want to serve?
<--- Score

48. How do you take a forward-looking perspective in identifying Web customer support research related to market response and models?
<--- Score

49. Who should resolve the Web customer support issues?
<--- Score

50. What resources or support might you need?
<--- Score

51. Do you need to avoid or amend any Web customer support activities?
<--- Score

52. What should be considered when identifying available resources, constraints, and deadlines?
<--- Score

53. Who needs budgets?
<--- Score

54. What are the expected benefits of Web customer support to the stakeholder?
<--- Score

55. Do you recognize Web customer support achievements?
<--- Score

56. What information do users need?
<--- Score

57. Will new equipment/products be required to facilitate Web customer support delivery, for example is new software needed?
<--- Score

58. What is the problem or issue?
<--- Score

59. What is the recognized need?
<--- Score

60. Are your goals realistic? Do you need to redefine your problem? Perhaps the problem has changed or

maybe you have reached your goal and need to set a new one?

<--- Score

61. For your Web customer support project, identify and describe the business environment, is there more than one layer to the business environment?

<--- Score

62. Consider your own Web customer support project, what types of organizational problems do you think might be causing or affecting your problem, based on the work done so far?

<--- Score

63. What are the Web customer support resources needed?

<--- Score

64. What Web customer support coordination do you need?

<--- Score

65. Which issues are too important to ignore?

<--- Score

66. What is the problem and/or vulnerability?

<--- Score

67. Who needs what information?

<--- Score

68. Looking at each person individually – does every one have the qualities which are needed to work in this group?

<--- Score

69. Is the need for organizational change recognized?

<--- Score

70. Is it needed?

<--- Score

71. Do you need different information or graphics?

<--- Score

72. Who needs to know about Web customer support?

<--- Score

73. Are there any specific expectations or concerns about the Web customer support team, Web customer support itself?

<--- Score

74. How does it fit into your organizational needs and tasks?

<--- Score

75. What creative shifts do you need to take?

<--- Score

76. Are employees recognized for desired behaviors?

<--- Score

77. What Web customer support problem should be solved?

<--- Score

78. Think about the people you identified for your Web customer support project and the project

responsibilities you would assign to them, what kind of training do you think they would need to perform these responsibilities effectively?
<--- Score

79. What would happen if Web customer support weren't done?
<--- Score

80. What needs to be done?
<--- Score

81. Where do you need to exercise leadership?
<--- Score

82. Are there any revenue recognition issues?
<--- Score

83. How are training requirements identified?
<--- Score

84. What else needs to be measured?
<--- Score

85. Does your organization need more Web customer support education?
<--- Score

86. How are you going to measure success?
<--- Score

87. Will it solve real problems?
<--- Score

88. What is the smallest subset of the problem you can usefully solve?

<--- Score

89. What is the extent or complexity of the Web customer support problem?
<--- Score

90. What extra resources will you need?
<--- Score

91. Is it clear when you think of the day ahead of you what activities and tasks you need to complete?
<--- Score

92. What prevents you from making the changes you know will make you a more effective Web customer support leader?
<--- Score

93. As a sponsor, customer or management, how important is it to meet goals, objectives?
<--- Score

94. Does Web customer support create potential expectations in other areas that need to be recognized and considered?
<--- Score

95. Which information does the Web customer support business case need to include?
<--- Score

96. To what extent would your organization benefit from being recognized as a award recipient?
<--- Score

97. What situation(s) led to this Web customer support Self Assessment?
<--- Score

Add up total points for this section:
_____ = Total points for this section

Divided by: _____ (number of statements answered) = _____
Average score for this section

Transfer your score to the Web customer support Index at the beginning of the Self-Assessment.

CRITERION #2: DEFINE:

INTENT: Formulate the stakeholder problem. Define the problem, needs and objectives.

In my belief, the answer to this question is clearly defined:

5 Strongly Agree

4 Agree

3 Neutral

2 Disagree

1 Strongly Disagree

1. What defines best in class?
<--- Score

2. Are customer(s) identified and segmented according to their different needs and requirements?
<--- Score

3. Is there a completed SIPOC representation, describing the Suppliers, Inputs, Process, Outputs, and

Customers?
<--- Score

4. What information do you gather?
<--- Score

5. What is the scope of Web customer support?
<--- Score

6. Is full participation by members in regularly held team meetings guaranteed?
<--- Score

7. Is the team formed and are team leaders (Coaches and Management Leads) assigned?
<--- Score

8. How would you define Web customer support leadership?
<--- Score

9. Has a team charter been developed and communicated?
<--- Score

10. What is in scope?
<--- Score

11. What is the worst case scenario?
<--- Score

12. Is the Web customer support scope manageable?
<--- Score

13. In what way can you redefine the criteria of choice clients have in your category in your favor?

<--- Score

14. Will team members regularly document their Web customer support work?
<--- Score

15. Is the team sponsored by a champion or stakeholder leader?
<--- Score

16. What Web customer support services do you require?
<--- Score

17. Is the current 'as is' process being followed? If not, what are the discrepancies?
<--- Score

18. Is it clearly defined in and to your organization what you do?
<--- Score

19. Have the customer needs been translated into specific, measurable requirements? How?
<--- Score

20. Has a high-level 'as is' process map been completed, verified and validated?
<--- Score

21. How are consistent Web customer support definitions important?
<--- Score

22. What is out-of-scope initially?
<--- Score

23. What sort of initial information to gather?
<--- Score

24. Is there a clear Web customer support case definition?
<--- Score

25. What is in the scope and what is not in scope?
<--- Score

26. How do you build the right business case?
<--- Score

27. When is the estimated completion date?
<--- Score

28. What was the context?
<--- Score

29. Has your scope been defined?
<--- Score

30. How can the value of Web customer support be defined?
<--- Score

31. What is a worst-case scenario for losses?
<--- Score

32. How will variation in the actual durations of each activity be dealt with to ensure that the expected Web customer support results are met?
<--- Score

33. Are roles and responsibilities formally defined?

<--- Score

34. Who are the Web customer support improvement team members, including Management Leads and Coaches?
<--- Score

35. What critical content must be communicated – who, what, when, where, and how?
<--- Score

36. What is the scope?
<--- Score

37. Have all basic functions of Web customer support been defined?
<--- Score

38. What customer feedback methods were used to solicit their input?
<--- Score

39. Is there a critical path to deliver Web customer support results?
<--- Score

40. When are meeting minutes sent out? Who is on the distribution list?
<--- Score

41. Has the Web customer support work been fairly and/or equitably divided and delegated among team members who are qualified and capable to perform the work? Has everyone contributed?
<--- Score

42. Has the improvement team collected the 'voice of the customer' (obtained feedback – qualitative and quantitative)?

<--- Score

43. What is the scope of the Web customer support work?

<--- Score

44. How would you define the culture at your organization, how susceptible is it to Web customer support changes?

<--- Score

45. Is the team adequately staffed with the desired cross-functionality? If not, what additional resources are available to the team?

<--- Score

46. The political context: who holds power?

<--- Score

47. Is the Web customer support scope complete and appropriately sized?

<--- Score

48. Has/have the customer(s) been identified?

<--- Score

49. How do you manage changes in Web customer support requirements?

<--- Score

50. What are the core elements of the Web customer support business case?

<--- Score

51. Who defines (or who defined) the rules and roles?
<--- Score

52. What are the Web customer support use cases?
<--- Score

**53. Will a Web customer support production
readiness review be required?**
<--- Score

54. What would be the goal or target for a Web
customer support's improvement team?
<--- Score

55. How do you gather requirements?
<--- Score

56. What are the Web customer support tasks and
definitions?
<--- Score

57. Are there different segments of customers?
<--- Score

58. Is Web customer support required?
<--- Score

59. How often are the team meetings?
<--- Score

60. Will team members perform Web customer
support work when assigned and in a timely fashion?
<--- Score

61. If substitutes have been appointed, have they

been briefed on the Web customer support goals and received regular communications as to the progress to date?
<--- Score

62. Are task requirements clearly defined?
<--- Score

63. Do you all define Web customer support in the same way?
<--- Score

64. Does the team have regular meetings?
<--- Score

65. How does the Web customer support manager ensure against scope creep?
<--- Score

66. Who is gathering Web customer support information?
<--- Score

67. Is the team equipped with available and reliable resources?
<--- Score

68. How will the Web customer support team and the group measure complete success of Web customer support?
<--- Score

69. Is the scope of Web customer support defined?
<--- Score

70. What sources do you use to gather information

for a Web customer support study?
<--- Score

71. What information should you gather?
<--- Score

72. What knowledge or experience is required?
<--- Score

73. Are accountability and ownership for Web customer support clearly defined?
<--- Score

74. Has anyone else (internal or external to the group) attempted to solve this problem or a similar one before? If so, what knowledge can be leveraged from these previous efforts?
<--- Score

75. What is out of scope?
<--- Score

76. What scope to assess?
<--- Score

77. What constraints exist that might impact the team?
<--- Score

78. How did the Web customer support manager receive input to the development of a Web customer support improvement plan and the estimated completion dates/times of each activity?
<--- Score

79. What intelligence can you gather?

<--- Score

80. Are approval levels defined for contracts and supplements to contracts?
<--- Score

81. How do you keep key subject matter experts in the loop?
<--- Score

82. What is the context?
<--- Score

83. How do you gather Web customer support requirements?
<--- Score

84. Are improvement team members fully trained on Web customer support?
<--- Score

85. Are the Web customer support requirements complete?
<--- Score

86. Are stakeholder processes mapped?
<--- Score

87. Have all of the relationships been defined properly?
<--- Score

88. What are the boundaries of the scope? What is in bounds and what is not? What is the start point? What is the stop point?
<--- Score

89. Are all requirements met?
<--- Score

90. Is scope creep really all bad news?
<--- Score

91. Is the improvement team aware of the different versions of a process: what they think it is vs. what it actually is vs. what it should be vs. what it could be?
<--- Score

92. What are the Roles and Responsibilities for each team member and its leadership? Where is this documented?
<--- Score

93. Are different versions of process maps needed to account for the different types of inputs?
<--- Score

94. Do the problem and goal statements meet the SMART criteria (specific, measurable, attainable, relevant, and time-bound)?
<--- Score

95. What scope do you want your strategy to cover?
<--- Score

96. Where can you gather more information?
<--- Score

97. Is there any additional Web customer support definition of success?
<--- Score

98. What baselines are required to be defined and managed?
<--- Score

99. Has the direction changed at all during the course of Web customer support? If so, when did it change and why?
<--- Score

100. Is there regularly 100% attendance at the team meetings? If not, have appointed substitutes attended to preserve cross-functionality and full representation?
<--- Score

101. Is Web customer support linked to key stakeholder goals and objectives?
<--- Score

102. Have specific policy objectives been defined?
<--- Score

103. What are the rough order estimates on cost savings/opportunities that Web customer support brings?
<--- Score

104. Are the Web customer support requirements testable?
<--- Score

105. Are required metrics defined, what are they?
<--- Score

106. Has everyone on the team, including the team leaders, been properly trained?

<--- Score

107. What specifically is the problem? Where does it occur? When does it occur? What is its extent?
<--- Score

108. What system do you use for gathering Web customer support information?
<--- Score

109. Has a Web customer support requirement not been met?
<--- Score

110. How have you defined all Web customer support requirements first?
<--- Score

111. How was the 'as is' process map developed, reviewed, verified and validated?
<--- Score

112. Who is gathering information?
<--- Score

113. Do you have a Web customer support success story or case study ready to tell and share?
<--- Score

114. What key stakeholder process output measure(s) does Web customer support leverage and how?
<--- Score

115. Is data collected and displayed to better understand customer(s) critical needs and requirements.

<--- Score

116. Has a project plan, Gantt chart, or similar been developed/completed?
<--- Score

117. How do you catch Web customer support definition inconsistencies?
<--- Score

118. When is/was the Web customer support start date?
<--- Score

119. How do you manage scope?
<--- Score

120. What is the definition of Web customer support excellence?
<--- Score

121. Are resources adequate for the scope?
<--- Score

122. How is the team tracking and documenting its work?
<--- Score

123. Does the scope remain the same?
<--- Score

124. Is there a completed, verified, and validated high-level 'as is' (not 'should be' or 'could be') stakeholder process map?
<--- Score

125. How do you think the partners involved in Web customer support would have defined success?
<--- Score

126. What are the tasks and definitions?
<--- Score

127. How and when will the baselines be defined?
<--- Score

128. What are (control) requirements for Web customer support Information?
<--- Score

129. Is there a Web customer support management charter, including stakeholder case, problem and goal statements, scope, milestones, roles and responsibilities, communication plan?
<--- Score

130. What is the definition of success?
<--- Score

131. Scope of sensitive information?
<--- Score

132. Who approved the Web customer support scope?
<--- Score

133. What gets examined?
<--- Score

134. What is the scope of the Web customer support effort?
<--- Score

135. What happens if Web customer support's scope changes?
<--- Score

136. Do you have organizational privacy requirements?
<--- Score

137. Are there any constraints known that bear on the ability to perform Web customer support work? How is the team addressing them?
<--- Score

138. What are the dynamics of the communication plan?
<--- Score

139. What are the compelling stakeholder reasons for embarking on Web customer support?
<--- Score

140. Is special Web customer support user knowledge required?
<--- Score

141. Are audit criteria, scope, frequency and methods defined?
<--- Score

142. Is Web customer support currently on schedule according to the plan?
<--- Score

Add up total points for this section:
_ _ _ _ _ = Total points for this section

Divided by: _____ (number of
statements answered) = _____
Average score for this section

Transfer your score to the Web customer
support Index at the beginning of the
Self-Assessment.

CRITERION #3: MEASURE:

INTENT: Gather the correct data.
Measure the current performance and
evolution of the situation.

In my belief, the answer to this
question is clearly defined:

5 Strongly Agree

4 Agree

3 Neutral

2 Disagree

1 Strongly Disagree

1. How are measurements made?
<--- Score

2. What measurements are being captured?
<--- Score

3. How to cause the change?
<--- Score

4. How do you measure lifecycle phases?
<--- Score

5. How do you prevent mis-estimating cost?
<--- Score

6. What can be used to verify compliance?
<--- Score

7. Where is the cost?
<--- Score

8. Does the Web customer support task fit the client's priorities?
<--- Score

9. Do you have a flow diagram of what happens?
<--- Score

10. What are the types and number of measures to use?
<--- Score

11. Do you effectively measure and reward individual and team performance?
<--- Score

12. Is it possible to estimate the impact of unanticipated complexity such as wrong or failed assumptions, feedback, etcetera on proposed reforms?
<--- Score

13. When a disaster occurs, who gets priority?
<--- Score

14. Among the Web customer support product and service cost to be estimated, which is considered hardest to estimate?
<--- Score

15. How do you quantify and qualify impacts?
<--- Score

16. What does a Test Case verify?
<--- Score

17. What drives O&M cost?
<--- Score

18. Do you have an issue in getting priority?
<--- Score

19. When are costs are incurred?
<--- Score

20. What are the operational costs after Web customer support deployment?
<--- Score

21. Where is it measured?
<--- Score

22. How do you verify the Web customer support requirements quality?
<--- Score

23. What do you measure and why?
<--- Score

24. Is the solution cost-effective?
<--- Score

25. When should you bother with diagrams?
<--- Score

26. Are the Web customer support benefits worth its costs?
<--- Score

27. What could cause you to change course?
<--- Score

28. What does losing customers cost your organization?
<--- Score

29. Why do you expend time and effort to implement measurement, for whom?
<--- Score

30. At what cost?
<--- Score

31. What are the costs of delaying Web customer support action?
<--- Score

32. What are the current costs of the Web customer support process?
<--- Score

33. How can you reduce costs?
<--- Score

34. How do you verify your resources?
<--- Score

35. Why do the measurements/indicators matter?
<--- Score

36. Is there an opportunity to verify requirements?
<--- Score

37. Are there any easy-to-implement alternatives to Web customer support? Sometimes other solutions are available that do not require the cost implications of a full-blown project?
<--- Score

38. What tests verify requirements?
<--- Score

39. How do you measure efficient delivery of Web customer support services?
<--- Score

40. What are hidden Web customer support quality costs?
<--- Score

41. What is your decision requirements diagram?
<--- Score

42. What are the estimated costs of proposed changes?
<--- Score

43. Are you taking your company in the direction of better and revenue or cheaper and cost?
<--- Score

44. What are your customers expectations and measures?

<--- Score

45. What are the Web customer support key cost drivers?
<--- Score

46. Do you have any cost Web customer support limitation requirements?
<--- Score

47. What is the total fixed cost?
<--- Score

48. What are the costs?
<--- Score

49. How much does it cost?
<--- Score

50. What does your operating model cost?
<--- Score

51. What are the Web customer support investment costs?
<--- Score

52. What methods are feasible and acceptable to estimate the impact of reforms?
<--- Score

53. Are there competing Web customer support priorities?
<--- Score

54. What could cause delays in the schedule?
<--- Score

55. How do you aggregate measures across priorities?
<--- Score

56. What are your key Web customer support organizational performance measures, including key short and longer-term financial measures?
<--- Score

57. How do you verify the authenticity of the data and information used?
<--- Score

58. How sensitive must the Web customer support strategy be to cost?
<--- Score

59. Are there measurements based on task performance?
<--- Score

60. How is progress measured?
<--- Score

61. Which measures and indicators matter?
<--- Score

62. Are Web customer support vulnerabilities categorized and prioritized?
<--- Score

63. Does a Web customer support quantification method exist?
<--- Score

64. Which Web customer support impacts are

significant?
<--- Score

65. How will costs be allocated?
<--- Score

66. How do you measure variability?
<--- Score

67. How will you measure your Web customer support effectiveness?
<--- Score

68. What potential environmental factors impact the Web customer support effort?
<--- Score

69. Do you aggressively reward and promote the people who have the biggest impact on creating excellent Web customer support services/products?
<--- Score

70. What causes mismanagement?
<--- Score

71. Who pays the cost?
<--- Score

72. What causes innovation to fail or succeed in your organization?
<--- Score

73. What are the costs of reform?
<--- Score

74. Was a business case (cost/benefit) developed?
<--- Score

75. How will your organization measure success?
<--- Score

76. How long to keep data and how to manage retention costs?
<--- Score

77. What is the cost of rework?
<--- Score

78. How are costs allocated?
<--- Score

79. What is the total cost related to deploying Web customer support, including any consulting or professional services?
<--- Score

80. Has a cost center been established?
<--- Score

81. How do you verify performance?
<--- Score

82. Are missed Web customer support opportunities costing your organization money?
<--- Score

83. What are the uncertainties surrounding estimates of impact?
<--- Score

84. How can a Web customer support test verify

your ideas or assumptions?
<--- Score

85. How can you measure Web customer support in a systematic way?
<--- Score

86. Are actual costs in line with budgeted costs?
<--- Score

87. Which costs should be taken into account?
<--- Score

88. Does management have the right priorities among projects?
<--- Score

89. What are your operating costs?
<--- Score

90. How will effects be measured?
<--- Score

91. What are the costs and benefits?
<--- Score

92. What harm might be caused?
<--- Score

93. How will measures be used to manage and adapt?
<--- Score

94. What would be a real cause for concern?
<--- Score

95. What happens if cost savings do not materialize?

<--- Score

96. What are the strategic priorities for this year?
<--- Score

97. What is the cause of any Web customer support gaps?
<--- Score

98. What disadvantage does this cause for the user?
<--- Score

99. Who should receive measurement reports?
<--- Score

100. Will Web customer support have an impact on current business continuity, disaster recovery processes and/or infrastructure?
<--- Score

101. Are the units of measure consistent?
<--- Score

102. How will success or failure be measured?
<--- Score

103. How is performance measured?
<--- Score

104. What is the root cause(s) of the problem?
<--- Score

105. What would it cost to replace your technology?
<--- Score

106. Have you included everything in your Web customer support cost models?
<--- Score

107. How do you control the overall costs of your work processes?
<--- Score

108. Is the cost worth the Web customer support effort ?
<--- Score

109. How do you verify and develop ideas and innovations?
<--- Score

110. How do your measurements capture actionable Web customer support information for use in exceeding your customers expectations and securing your customers engagement?
<--- Score

111. What details are required of the Web customer support cost structure?
<--- Score

112. How frequently do you track Web customer support measures?
<--- Score

113. Are indirect costs charged to the Web customer support program?
<--- Score

114. What are your primary costs, revenues,

assets?
<--- Score

115. What measurements are possible, practicable and meaningful?
<--- Score

116. What causes investor action?
<--- Score

117. Are supply costs steady or fluctuating?
<--- Score

118. Are you able to realize any cost savings?
<--- Score

119. What causes extra work or rework?
<--- Score

120. What relevant entities could be measured?
<--- Score

121. What are allowable costs?
<--- Score

122. Are you aware of what could cause a problem?
<--- Score

123. How can you measure the performance?
<--- Score

124. Do the benefits outweigh the costs?
<--- Score

125. What is the Web customer support business impact?

<--- Score

126. Did you tackle the cause or the symptom?
<--- Score

127. How is the value delivered by Web customer support being measured?
<--- Score

128. How will you measure success?
<--- Score

129. What do people want to verify?
<--- Score

130. What is your Web customer support quality cost segregation study?
<--- Score

131. Have design-to-cost goals been established?
<--- Score

132. What is measured? Why?
<--- Score

133. Are the measurements objective?
<--- Score

134. What evidence is there and what is measured?
<--- Score

135. How can you reduce the costs of obtaining inputs?
<--- Score

Add up total points for this section:

_____ = Total points for this section

Divided by: _____ (number of
statements answered) = _____
Average score for this section

Transfer your score to the Web customer
support Index at the beginning of the
Self-Assessment.

CRITERION #4: ANALYZE:

INTENT: Analyze causes, assumptions
and hypotheses.

In my belief, the answer to this
question is clearly defined:

5 Strongly Agree

4 Agree

3 Neutral

2 Disagree

1 Strongly Disagree

1. Are all staff in core Web customer support subjects
Highly Qualified?
<--- Score

2. Who owns what data?
<--- Score

3. What will drive Web customer support change?
<--- Score

4. What are evaluation criteria for the output?
<--- Score

5. Who will facilitate the team and process?
<--- Score

6. What is the oversight process?
<--- Score

7. What qualifications are necessary?
<--- Score

8. What conclusions were drawn from the team's data collection and analysis? How did the team reach these conclusions?
<--- Score

9. How is the Web customer support Value Stream Mapping managed?
<--- Score

10. What are the personnel training and qualifications required?
<--- Score

11. How do you identify specific Web customer support investment opportunities and emerging trends?
<--- Score

12. Do your leaders quickly bounce back from setbacks?
<--- Score

13. What are your outputs?
<--- Score

14. How do you implement and manage your work processes to ensure that they meet design requirements?
<--- Score

15. What are your current levels and trends in key Web customer support measures or indicators of product and process performance that are important to and directly serve your customers?
<--- Score

16. How has the Web customer support data been gathered?
<--- Score

17. What information qualified as important?
<--- Score

18. What were the financial benefits resulting from any 'ground fruit or low-hanging fruit' (quick fixes)?
<--- Score

19. Has data output been validated?
<--- Score

20. What other jobs or tasks affect the performance of the steps in the Web customer support process?
<--- Score

21. What do you need to qualify?
<--- Score

22. Is data and process analysis, root cause analysis and quantifying the gap/opportunity in place?
<--- Score

23. Who is involved in the management review process?
<--- Score

24. What successful thing are you doing today that may be blinding you to new growth opportunities?
<--- Score

25. Is the performance gap determined?
<--- Score

26. Are your outputs consistent?
<--- Score

27. What qualifies as competition?
<--- Score

28. What other organizational variables, such as reward systems or communication systems, affect the performance of this Web customer support process?
<--- Score

29. Is there a strict change management process?
<--- Score

30. Was a detailed process map created to amplify critical steps of the 'as is' stakeholder process?
<--- Score

31. Do your employees have the opportunity to do what they do best everyday?
<--- Score

32. What are the revised rough estimates of the

financial savings/opportunity for Web customer support improvements?
<--- Score

33. Are Web customer support changes recognized early enough to be approved through the regular process?
<--- Score

34. Did any additional data need to be collected?
<--- Score

35. How will the Web customer support data be captured?
<--- Score

36. What is the cost of poor quality as supported by the team's analysis?
<--- Score

37. What types of data do your Web customer support indicators require?
<--- Score

38. Is the Web customer support process severely broken such that a re-design is necessary?
<--- Score

39. Is there any way to speed up the process?
<--- Score

40. Are you missing Web customer support opportunities?
<--- Score

41. What process should you select for improvement?

<--- Score

42. How was the detailed process map generated, verified, and validated?
<--- Score

43. How is Web customer support data gathered?
<--- Score

44. What are the best opportunities for value improvement?
<--- Score

45. What qualifications are needed?
<--- Score

46. Who will gather what data?
<--- Score

47. How many input/output points does it require?
<--- Score

48. What data do you need to collect?
<--- Score

49. How can risk management be tied procedurally to process elements?
<--- Score

50. Do several people in different organizational units assist with the Web customer support process?
<--- Score

51. Identify an operational issue in your organization, for example, could a particular task

be done more quickly or more efficiently by Web customer support?

<--- Score

52. Is the required Web customer support data gathered?

<--- Score

53. What is the complexity of the output produced?

<--- Score

54. How do your work systems and key work processes relate to and capitalize on your core competencies?

<--- Score

55. How do you ensure that the Web customer support opportunity is realistic?

<--- Score

56. Were any designed experiments used to generate additional insight into the data analysis?

<--- Score

57. Record-keeping requirements flow from the records needed as inputs, outputs, controls and for transformation of a Web customer support process, are the records needed as inputs to the Web customer support process available?

<--- Score

58. What tools were used to narrow the list of possible causes?

<--- Score

59. Think about some of the processes you undertake

within your organization, which do you own?
<--- Score

60. Which Web customer support data should be retained?
<--- Score

61. What kind of crime could a potential new hire have committed that would not only not disqualify him/her from being hired by your organization, but would actually indicate that he/she might be a particularly good fit?
<--- Score

62. Were Pareto charts (or similar) used to portray the 'heavy hitters' (or key sources of variation)?
<--- Score

63. What did the team gain from developing a sub-process map?
<--- Score

64. What, related to, Web customer support processes does your organization outsource?
<--- Score

65. How often will data be collected for measures?
<--- Score

66. Do quality systems drive continuous improvement?
<--- Score

67. What are the Web customer support business drivers?
<--- Score

68. A compounding model resolution with available relevant data can often provide insight towards a solution methodology; which Web customer support models, tools and techniques are necessary?

<--- Score

69. What resources go in to get the desired output?
<--- Score

70. Is the final output clearly identified?
<--- Score

71. How will the data be checked for quality?
<--- Score

72. What are your key performance measures or indicators and in-process measures for the control and improvement of your Web customer support processes?
<--- Score

73. How will the change process be managed?
<--- Score

74. What output to create?
<--- Score

75. How do you promote understanding that opportunity for improvement is not criticism of the status quo, or the people who created the status quo?
<--- Score

76. What qualifications and skills do you need?
<--- Score

77. Have the problem and goal statements been updated to reflect the additional knowledge gained from the analyze phase?
<--- Score

78. Have any additional benefits been identified that will result from closing all or most of the gaps?
<--- Score

79. Where is Web customer support data gathered?
<--- Score

80. Are gaps between current performance and the goal performance identified?
<--- Score

81. Who qualifies to gain access to data?
<--- Score

82. Should you invest in industry-recognized qualifications?
<--- Score

83. Where is the data coming from to measure compliance?
<--- Score

84. What controls do you have in place to protect data?
<--- Score

85. What quality tools were used to get through the analyze phase?
<--- Score

86. Can you add value to the current Web customer support decision-making process (largely qualitative) by incorporating uncertainty modeling (more quantitative)?
<--- Score

87. What Web customer support data will be collected?
<--- Score

88. What tools were used to generate the list of possible causes?
<--- Score

89. Where can you get qualified talent today?
<--- Score

90. Is the gap/opportunity displayed and communicated in financial terms?
<--- Score

91. What are the Web customer support design outputs?
<--- Score

92. What are your current levels and trends in key measures or indicators of Web customer support product and process performance that are important to and directly serve your customers? How do these results compare with the performance of your competitors and other organizations with similar offerings?
<--- Score

93. What are the disruptive Web customer support technologies that enable your organization to

radically change your business processes?
<--- Score

94. What is the Value Stream Mapping?
<--- Score

95. What is the output?
<--- Score

96. Did any value-added analysis or 'lean thinking' take place to identify some of the gaps shown on the 'as is' process map?
<--- Score

97. What internal processes need improvement?
<--- Score

98. Who gets your output?
<--- Score

99. Was a cause-and-effect diagram used to explore the different types of causes (or sources of variation)?
<--- Score

100. Do you understand your management processes today?
<--- Score

101. Think about the functions involved in your Web customer support project, what processes flow from these functions?
<--- Score

102. How are outputs preserved and protected?
<--- Score

103. How is data used for program management and improvement?

<--- Score

104. What systems/processes must you excel at?

<--- Score

105. What is the Web customer support Driver?

<--- Score

106. What does the data say about the performance of the stakeholder process?

<--- Score

107. Do you have the authority to produce the output?

<--- Score

108. Has an output goal been set?

<--- Score

109. Were there any improvement opportunities identified from the process analysis?

<--- Score

110. How do mission and objectives affect the Web customer support processes of your organization?

<--- Score

111. An organizationally feasible system request is one that considers the mission, goals and objectives of the organization, key questions are: is the Web customer support solution request practical and will it solve a problem or take advantage of an opportunity to achieve company goals?

<--- Score

112. Are all team members qualified for all tasks?
<--- Score

113. How will corresponding data be collected?
<--- Score

114. Do you, as a leader, bounce back quickly from setbacks?
<--- Score

115. What is your organizations system for selecting qualified vendors?
<--- Score

116. Do your contracts/agreements contain data security obligations?
<--- Score

117. Do staff qualifications match your project?
<--- Score

118. What were the crucial 'moments of truth' on the process map?
<--- Score

119. What process improvements will be needed?
<--- Score

120. Is the suppliers process defined and controlled?
<--- Score

121. How is the way you as the leader think and process information affecting your organizational

culture?

<--- Score

122. What training and qualifications will you need?

<--- Score

123. How does the organization define, manage, and improve its Web customer support processes?

<--- Score

124. How do you measure the operational performance of your key work systems and processes, including productivity, cycle time, and other appropriate measures of process effectiveness, efficiency, and innovation?

<--- Score

125. What data is gathered?

<--- Score

126. What qualifications do Web customer support leaders need?

<--- Score

127. What are the necessary qualifications?

<--- Score

128. What are your Web customer support processes?

<--- Score

129. What methods do you use to gather Web customer support data?

<--- Score

130. Is pre-qualification of suppliers carried out?

<--- Score

Add up total points for this section:
_____ = Total points for this section

Divided by: _____ (number of
statements answered) = _____
Average score for this section

Transfer your score to the Web customer
support Index at the beginning of the
Self-Assessment.

CRITERION #5: IMPROVE:

INTENT: Develop a practical solution. Innovate, establish and test the solution and to measure the results.

In my belief, the answer to this question is clearly defined:

5 Strongly Agree

4 Agree

3 Neutral

2 Disagree

1 Strongly Disagree

1. How do you go about comparing Web customer support approaches/solutions?
<--- Score

2. What error proofing will be done to address some of the discrepancies observed in the 'as is' process?
<--- Score

3. How can the phases of Web customer support

development be identified?

<--- Score

4. What risks do you need to manage?

<--- Score

5. How do you mitigate Web customer support risk?

<--- Score

6. How can skill-level changes improve Web customer support?

<--- Score

7. Is there a high likelihood that any recommendations will achieve their intended results?

<--- Score

8. What current systems have to be understood and/or changed?

<--- Score

9. Will the controls trigger any other risks?

<--- Score

10. What tools were used to tap into the creativity and encourage 'outside the box' thinking?

<--- Score

11. How do you link measurement and risk?

<--- Score

12. How risky is your organization?

<--- Score

13. What practices helps your organization to develop

its capacity to recognize patterns?
<--- Score

14. What are your current levels and trends in key measures or indicators of workforce and leader development?
<--- Score

15. How does the team improve its work?
<--- Score

16. What actually has to improve and by how much?
<--- Score

17. Is the Web customer support documentation thorough?
<--- Score

18. How is knowledge sharing about risk management improved?
<--- Score

19. Which of the recognised risks out of all risks can be most likely transferred?
<--- Score

20. Have you achieved Web customer support improvements?
<--- Score

21. What strategies for Web customer support improvement are successful?
<--- Score

22. What is Web customer support's impact on utilizing the best solution(s)?

<--- Score

23. In the past few months, what is the smallest change you have made that has had the biggest positive result? What was it about that small change that produced the large return?
<--- Score

24. How significant is the improvement in the eyes of the end user?
<--- Score

25. How do you improve your likelihood of success ?
<--- Score

26. How risky is your organization?
<--- Score

27. How do you improve Web customer support service perception, and satisfaction?
<--- Score

28. Risk factors: what are the characteristics of Web customer support that make it risky?
<--- Score

29. Can the solution be designed and implemented within an acceptable time period?
<--- Score

30. Was a Web customer support charter developed?
<--- Score

31. How will you measure the results?
<--- Score

32. How can you improve performance?
<--- Score

33. Who are the key stakeholders for the Web customer support evaluation?
<--- Score

34. What do you want to improve?
<--- Score

35. Do those selected for the Web customer support team have a good general understanding of what Web customer support is all about?
<--- Score

36. What were the criteria for evaluating a Web customer support pilot?
<--- Score

37. How do you measure progress and evaluate training effectiveness?
<--- Score

38. Risk Identification: What are the possible risk events your organization faces in relation to Web customer support?
<--- Score

39. Who do you report Web customer support results to?
<--- Score

40. How will you know when its improved?
<--- Score

41. Is any Web customer support documentation required?

<--- Score

42. What is the team's contingency plan for potential problems occurring in implementation?

<--- Score

43. Do vendor agreements bring new compliance risk ?

<--- Score

44. What were the underlying assumptions on the cost-benefit analysis?

<--- Score

45. Who manages Web customer support risk?

<--- Score

46. Web customer support risk decisions: whose call Is It?

<--- Score

47. How do you manage Web customer support risk?

<--- Score

48. What criteria will you use to assess your Web customer support risks?

<--- Score

49. Does a good decision guarantee a good outcome?

<--- Score

50. What tools were most useful during the improve phase?

<--- Score

51. How do you measure risk?
<--- Score

52. Explorations of the frontiers of Web customer support will help you build influence, improve Web customer support, optimize decision making, and sustain change, what is your approach?
<--- Score

53. How do you improve productivity?
<--- Score

54. Is risk periodically assessed?
<--- Score

55. How does your organization evaluate strategic Web customer support success?
<--- Score

56. What are the concrete Web customer support results?
<--- Score

57. Is the solution technically practical?
<--- Score

58. Would you develop a Web customer support Communication Strategy?
<--- Score

59. What improvements have been achieved?
<--- Score

60. Are the risks fully understood, reasonable and

manageable?
<--- Score

61. How will you know that you have improved?
<--- Score

62. What assumptions are made about the solution and approach?
<--- Score

63. What Web customer support improvements can be made?
<--- Score

64. What is the risk?
<--- Score

65. At what point will vulnerability assessments be performed once Web customer support is put into production (e.g., ongoing Risk Management after implementation)?
<--- Score

66. What tools do you use once you have decided on a Web customer support strategy and more importantly how do you choose?
<--- Score

67. Is the measure of success for Web customer support understandable to a variety of people?
<--- Score

68. Who are the Web customer support decision makers?
<--- Score

69. Can you identify any significant risks or exposures to Web customer support third- parties (vendors, service providers, alliance partners etc) that concern you?
<--- Score

70. Where do the Web customer support decisions reside?
<--- Score

71. What to do with the results or outcomes of measurements?
<--- Score

72. What is the magnitude of the improvements?
<--- Score

73. What resources are required for the improvement efforts?
<--- Score

74. Are you assessing Web customer support and risk?
<--- Score

75. What lessons, if any, from a pilot were incorporated into the design of the full-scale solution?
<--- Score

76. How will you recognize and celebrate results?
<--- Score

77. Who will be responsible for making the decisions to include or exclude requested changes once Web customer support is underway?
<--- Score

78. Is the Web customer support risk managed?
<--- Score

79. How do you manage and improve your Web customer support work systems to deliver customer value and achieve organizational success and sustainability?
<--- Score

80. How do you decide how much to remunerate an employee?
<--- Score

81. Which Web customer support solution is appropriate?
<--- Score

82. What are the affordable Web customer support risks?
<--- Score

83. How can you improve Web customer support?
<--- Score

84. Is the scope clearly documented?
<--- Score

85. What is the implementation plan?
<--- Score

86. How will you know that a change is an improvement?
<--- Score

87. How is continuous improvement applied to risk

management?
<--- Score

88. Risk events: what are the things that could go wrong?
<--- Score

89. Who should make the Web customer support decisions?
<--- Score

90. Who do you report Web customer support results to?
<--- Score

91. Are the most efficient solutions problem-specific?
<--- Score

92. What can you do to improve?
<--- Score

93. Do you cover the five essential competencies: Communication, Collaboration,Innovation, Adaptability, and Leadership that improve an organizations ability to leverage the new Web customer support in a volatile global economy?
<--- Score

94. Who are the Web customer support decision-makers?
<--- Score

95. Why improve in the first place?
<--- Score

96. What are the expected Web customer support

results?

<--- Score

97. Are risk triggers captured?

<--- Score

98. What needs improvement? Why?

<--- Score

99. Who are the people involved in developing and implementing Web customer support?

<--- Score

100. For decision problems, how do you develop a decision statement?

<--- Score

101. What area needs the greatest improvement?

<--- Score

102. What tools were used to evaluate the potential solutions?

<--- Score

103. For estimation problems, how do you develop an estimation statement?

<--- Score

104. What went well, what should change, what can improve?

<--- Score

105. If you could go back in time five years, what decision would you make differently? What is your best guess as to what decision you're making today you might regret five years from now?

<--- Score

106. How scalable is your Web customer support solution?
<--- Score

107. Are risk management tasks balanced centrally and locally?
<--- Score

108. Are decisions made in a timely manner?
<--- Score

109. Do you need to do a usability evaluation?
<--- Score

110. How do you keep improving Web customer support?
<--- Score

111. How can you better manage risk?
<--- Score

112. Who manages supplier risk management in your organization?
<--- Score

113. How are Web customer support risks managed?
<--- Score

114. What alternative responses are available to manage risk?
<--- Score

115. How do you measure improved Web customer

support service perception, and satisfaction?
<--- Score

116. Do you combine technical expertise with business knowledge and Web customer support Key topics include lifecycles, development approaches, requirements and how to make a business case?
<--- Score

117. Is Web customer support documentation maintained?
<--- Score

118. Who will be responsible for documenting the Web customer support requirements in detail?
<--- Score

119. Are the key business and technology risks being managed?
<--- Score

120. Who will be using the results of the measurement activities?
<--- Score

121. Is the Web customer support solution sustainable?
<--- Score

122. How are policy decisions made and where?
<--- Score

123. Are procedures documented for managing Web customer support risks?
<--- Score

124. Who controls key decisions that will be made?
<--- Score

125. Can you integrate quality management and risk management?
<--- Score

126. Are events managed to resolution?
<--- Score

127. Is supporting Web customer support documentation required?
<--- Score

128. Have you identified breakpoints and/or risk tolerances that will trigger broad consideration of a potential need for intervention or modification of strategy?
<--- Score

129. How do you define the solutions' scope?
<--- Score

130. What are the Web customer support security risks?
<--- Score

Add up total points for this section:
_ _ _ _ _ = Total points for this section

Divided by: _ _ _ _ _ _ (number of
statements answered) = _ _ _ _ _ _
Average score for this section

Transfer your score to the Web customer
support Index at the beginning of the

Self-Assessment.

CRITERION #6: CONTROL:

INTENT: Implement the practical solution. Maintain the performance and correct possible complications.

In my belief, the answer to this question is clearly defined:

5 Strongly Agree

4 Agree

3 Neutral

2 Disagree

1 Strongly Disagree

1. How can you best use all of your knowledge repositories to enhance learning and sharing?
<--- Score

2. How do you encourage people to take control and responsibility?
<--- Score

3. Are pertinent alerts monitored, analyzed and

distributed to appropriate personnel?
<--- Score

4. Who has control over resources?
<--- Score

5. Has the Web customer support value of standards been quantified?
<--- Score

6. Who controls critical resources?
<--- Score

7. Does Web customer support appropriately measure and monitor risk?
<--- Score

8. Is a response plan established and deployed?
<--- Score

9. Against what alternative is success being measured?
<--- Score

10. Is there a standardized process?
<--- Score

11. Are new process steps, standards, and documentation ingrained into normal operations?
<--- Score

12. How will the process owner verify improvement in present and future sigma levels, process capabilities?
<--- Score

13. Does job training on the documented procedures

need to be part of the process team's education and training?

<--- Score

14. What can you control?

<--- Score

15. Is there a recommended audit plan for routine surveillance inspections of Web customer support's gains?

<--- Score

16. Is there an action plan in case of emergencies?

<--- Score

17. You may have created your quality measures at a time when you lacked resources, technology wasn't up to the required standard, or low service levels were the industry norm. Have those circumstances changed?

<--- Score

18. Do the viable solutions scale to future needs?

<--- Score

19. Who sets the Web customer support standards?

<--- Score

20. Are the planned controls working?

<--- Score

21. How might the group capture best practices and lessons learned so as to leverage improvements?

<--- Score

22. What do you measure to verify effectiveness

gains?
<--- Score

23. How do you plan for the cost of succession?
<--- Score

24. Is there a Web customer support Communication plan covering who needs to get what information when?
<--- Score

25. Are operating procedures consistent?
<--- Score

26. Who will be in control?
<--- Score

27. Can you adapt and adjust to changing Web customer support situations?
<--- Score

28. Who is going to spread your message?
<--- Score

29. Does a troubleshooting guide exist or is it needed?
<--- Score

30. What is the control/monitoring plan?
<--- Score

31. How is Web customer support project cost planned, managed, monitored?
<--- Score

32. Are the planned controls in place?
<--- Score

33. What other areas of the group might benefit from the Web customer support team's improvements, knowledge, and learning?
<--- Score

34. What adjustments to the strategies are needed?
<--- Score

35. Who is the Web customer support process owner?
<--- Score

36. Is there a control plan in place for sustaining improvements (short and long-term)?
<--- Score

37. What do you stand for--and what are you against?
<--- Score

38. In the case of a Web customer support project, the criteria for the audit derive from implementation objectives, an audit of a Web customer support project involves assessing whether the recommendations outlined for implementation have been met, can you track that any Web customer support project is implemented as planned, and is it working?
<--- Score

39. Is knowledge gained on process shared and institutionalized?
<--- Score

40. Do you monitor the effectiveness of your Web

customer support activities?
<--- Score

41. What are your results for key measures or indicators of the accomplishment of your Web customer support strategy and action plans, including building and strengthening core competencies?
<--- Score

42. Have new or revised work instructions resulted?
<--- Score

43. Do you monitor the Web customer support decisions made and fine tune them as they evolve?
<--- Score

44. Will the team be available to assist members in planning investigations?
<--- Score

45. Can support from partners be adjusted?
<--- Score

46. How do senior leaders actions reflect a commitment to the organizations Web customer support values?
<--- Score

47. How will input, process, and output variables be checked to detect for sub-optimal conditions?
<--- Score

48. Where do ideas that reach policy makers and planners as proposals for Web customer support strengthening and reform actually originate?
<--- Score

49. What other systems, operations, processes, and infrastructures (hiring practices, staffing, training, incentives/rewards, metrics/dashboards/scorecards, etc.) need updates, additions, changes, or deletions in order to facilitate knowledge transfer and improvements?
<--- Score

50. What key inputs and outputs are being measured on an ongoing basis?
<--- Score

51. Are documented procedures clear and easy to follow for the operators?
<--- Score

52. What is the standard for acceptable Web customer support performance?
<--- Score

53. Will existing staff require re-training, for example, to learn new business processes?
<--- Score

54. Implementation Planning: is a pilot needed to test the changes before a full roll out occurs?
<--- Score

55. What are the known security controls?
<--- Score

56. Are controls in place and consistently applied?
<--- Score

57. How will the process owner and team be able to

hold the gains?
<--- Score

58. What are the key elements of your Web customer support performance improvement system, including your evaluation, organizational learning, and innovation processes?
<--- Score

59. Is the Web customer support test/monitoring cost justified?
<--- Score

60. Is there a documented and implemented monitoring plan?
<--- Score

61. Is new knowledge gained imbedded in the response plan?
<--- Score

62. How widespread is its use?
<--- Score

63. What is your theory of human motivation, and how does your compensation plan fit with that view?
<--- Score

64. What are the performance and scale of the Web customer support tools?
<--- Score

65. Has the improved process and its steps been standardized?
<--- Score

66. What should the next improvement project be that is related to Web customer support?
<--- Score

67. What is the best design framework for Web customer support organization now that, in a post industrial-age if the top-down, command and control model is no longer relevant?
<--- Score

68. How will report readings be checked to effectively monitor performance?
<--- Score

69. What are you attempting to measure/monitor?
<--- Score

70. How do you plan on providing proper recognition and disclosure of supporting companies?
<--- Score

71. Act/Adjust: What Do you Need to Do Differently?
<--- Score

72. Is a response plan in place for when the input, process, or output measures indicate an 'out-of-control' condition?
<--- Score

73. How likely is the current Web customer support plan to come in on schedule or on budget?
<--- Score

74. Are suggested corrective/restorative actions indicated on the response plan for known causes to

problems that might surface?
<--- Score

75. Is there a transfer of ownership and knowledge to process owner and process team tasked with the responsibilities.
<--- Score

76. What are the critical parameters to watch?
<--- Score

77. How do you select, collect, align, and integrate Web customer support data and information for tracking daily operations and overall organizational performance, including progress relative to strategic objectives and action plans?
<--- Score

78. Are the Web customer support standards challenging?
<--- Score

79. Are there documented procedures?
<--- Score

80. How will you measure your QA plan's effectiveness?
<--- Score

81. What Web customer support standards are applicable?
<--- Score

82. How do controls support value?
<--- Score

83. How do your controls stack up?
<--- Score

84. Does the response plan contain a definite closed loop continual improvement scheme (e.g., plan-do-check-act)?
<--- Score

85. How is change control managed?
<--- Score

86. Are you measuring, monitoring and predicting Web customer support activities to optimize operations and profitability, and enhancing outcomes?
<--- Score

87. What do your reports reflect?
<--- Score

88. How do you establish and deploy modified action plans if circumstances require a shift in plans and rapid execution of new plans?
<--- Score

89. Will any special training be provided for results interpretation?
<--- Score

90. Is reporting being used or needed?
<--- Score

91. How will the day-to-day responsibilities for monitoring and continual improvement be transferred from the improvement team to the process owner?

<--- Score

92. How will Web customer support decisions be made and monitored?
<--- Score

93. How will new or emerging customer needs/ requirements be checked/communicated to orient the process toward meeting the new specifications and continually reducing variation?
<--- Score

94. What are customers monitoring?
<--- Score

95. Does the Web customer support performance meet the customer's requirements?
<--- Score

96. What is the recommended frequency of auditing?
<--- Score

97. What quality tools were useful in the control phase?
<--- Score

98. How do you spread information?
<--- Score

99. Do the Web customer support decisions you make today help people and the planet tomorrow?
<--- Score

100. Is there documentation that will support the successful operation of the improvement?
<--- Score

101. Will your goals reflect your program budget?
<--- Score

Add up total points for this section:
_ _ _ _ _ = Total points for this section

Divided by: _ _ _ _ _ _ (number of
statements answered) = _ _ _ _ _ _
Average score for this section

Transfer your score to the Web customer
support Index at the beginning of the
Self-Assessment.

CRITERION #7: SUSTAIN:

INTENT: Retain the benefits.

In my belief, the answer to this question is clearly defined:

5 Strongly Agree

4 Agree

3 Neutral

2 Disagree

1 Strongly Disagree

1. What was the last experiment you ran?
<--- Score

2. What are your most important goals for the strategic Web customer support objectives?
<--- Score

3. How do you transition from the baseline to the target?
<--- Score

4. How do you manage Web customer support Knowledge Management (KM)?
<--- Score

5. Are you relevant? Will you be relevant five years from now? Ten?
<--- Score

6. Where can you break convention?
<--- Score

7. What are the challenges?
<--- Score

8. What is your BATNA (best alternative to a negotiated agreement)?
<--- Score

9. Is your strategy driving your strategy? Or is the way in which you allocate resources driving your strategy?
<--- Score

10. Would you rather sell to knowledgeable and informed customers or to uninformed customers?
<--- Score

11. At what moment would you think; Will I get fired?
<--- Score

12. Is your basic point _____ or _____?
<--- Score

13. What knowledge, skills and characteristics mark a good Web customer support project manager?
<--- Score

14. Do you have the right capabilities and capacities?
<--- Score

15. Is a Web customer support team work effort in place?
<--- Score

16. Is there a work around that you can use?
<--- Score

17. How do you determine the key elements that affect Web customer support workforce satisfaction, how are these elements determined for different workforce groups and segments?
<--- Score

18. What do we do when new problems arise?
<--- Score

19. What are the business goals Web customer support is aiming to achieve?
<--- Score

20. Did your employees make progress today?
<--- Score

21. Are you paying enough attention to the partners your company depends on to succeed?
<--- Score

22. What are strategies for increasing support and reducing opposition?
<--- Score

23. Can you do all this work?

<--- Score

24. Are there any activities that you can take off your to do list?
<--- Score

25. Is Web customer support dependent on the successful delivery of a current project?
<--- Score

26. What information is critical to your organization that your executives are ignoring?
<--- Score

27. Which models, tools and techniques are necessary?
<--- Score

28. What is an unauthorized commitment?
<--- Score

29. How do you make it meaningful in connecting Web customer support with what users do day-to-day?
<--- Score

30. Whom among your colleagues do you trust, and for what?
<--- Score

31. What are the success criteria that will indicate that Web customer support objectives have been met and the benefits delivered?
<--- Score

32. What management system can you use to

leverage the Web customer support experience, ideas, and concerns of the people closest to the work to be done?

<--- Score

33. Who do you think the world wants your organization to be?

<--- Score

34. Who is responsible for Web customer support?

<--- Score

35. Who do we want your customers to become?

<--- Score

36. If you were responsible for initiating and implementing major changes in your organization, what steps might you take to ensure acceptance of those changes?

<--- Score

37. How do you track customer value, profitability or financial return, organizational success, and sustainability?

<--- Score

38. Is there any existing Web customer support governance structure?

<--- Score

39. What trouble can you get into?

<--- Score

40. What is the kind of project structure that would be appropriate for your Web customer support project, should it be formal and complex, or can it

be less formal and relatively simple?
<--- Score

41. If no one would ever find out about your accomplishments, how would you lead differently?
<--- Score

42. What role does communication play in the success or failure of a Web customer support project?
<--- Score

43. How do you foster innovation?
<--- Score

44. If your customer were your grandmother, would you tell her to buy what you're selling?
<--- Score

45. What Web customer support modifications can you make work for you?
<--- Score

46. How do you set Web customer support stretch targets and how do you get people to not only participate in setting these stretch targets but also that they strive to achieve these?
<--- Score

47. Who do you want your customers to become?
<--- Score

48. Do Web customer support rules make a reasonable demand on a users capabilities?
<--- Score

49. What are you trying to prove to yourself, and how might it be hijacking your life and business success?
<--- Score

50. How much does Web customer support help?
<--- Score

51. Who will be responsible for deciding whether Web customer support goes ahead or not after the initial investigations?
<--- Score

52. Who have you, as a company, historically been when you've been at your best?
<--- Score

53. How is implementation research currently incorporated into each of your goals?
<--- Score

54. Are you / should you be revolutionary or evolutionary?
<--- Score

55. Do you think you know, or do you know you know ?
<--- Score

56. Who are your customers?
<--- Score

57. Who is responsible for ensuring appropriate resources (time, people and money) are allocated to Web customer support?
<--- Score

58. What is the recommended frequency of auditing?
<--- Score

59. Who are four people whose careers you have enhanced?
<--- Score

60. How do you engage the workforce, in addition to satisfying them?
<--- Score

61. What must you excel at?
<--- Score

62. How are you doing compared to your industry?
<--- Score

63. What is effective Web customer support?
<--- Score

64. How do customers see your organization?
<--- Score

65. How do senior leaders deploy your organizations vision and values through your leadership system, to the workforce, to key suppliers and partners, and to customers and other stakeholders, as appropriate?
<--- Score

66. What threat is Web customer support addressing?
<--- Score

67. What would you recommend your friend do if he/she were facing this dilemma?
<--- Score

68. Why should you adopt a Web customer support framework?

<--- Score

69. What trophy do you want on your mantle?

<--- Score

70. How do you provide a safe environment -physically and emotionally?

<--- Score

71. Who are the key stakeholders?

<--- Score

72. Are assumptions made in Web customer support stated explicitly?

<--- Score

73. In a project to restructure Web customer support outcomes, which stakeholders would you involve?

<--- Score

74. How do you keep records, of what?

<--- Score

75. Will there be any necessary staff changes (redundancies or new hires)?

<--- Score

76. What business benefits will Web customer support goals deliver if achieved?

<--- Score

77. If your company went out of business tomorrow, would anyone who doesn't get a paycheck here care?

<--- Score

78. What are the rules and assumptions your industry operates under? What if the opposite were true?
<--- Score

79. Operational - will it work?
<--- Score

80. How do you assess the Web customer support pitfalls that are inherent in implementing it?
<--- Score

81. Were lessons learned captured and communicated?
<--- Score

82. How do you foster the skills, knowledge, talents, attributes, and characteristics you want to have?
<--- Score

83. Have new benefits been realized?
<--- Score

84. What will be the consequences to the stakeholder (financial, reputation etc) if Web customer support does not go ahead or fails to deliver the objectives?
<--- Score

85. What is the source of the strategies for Web customer support strengthening and reform?
<--- Score

86. Do you know what you are doing? And who do you call if you don't?

<--- Score

87. Who is responsible for errors?
<--- Score

88. Who will determine interim and final deadlines?
<--- Score

89. Which functions and people interact with the supplier and or customer?
<--- Score

90. Can you break it down?
<--- Score

91. What are specific Web customer support rules to follow?
<--- Score

92. If you had to rebuild your organization without any traditional competitive advantages (i.e., no killer technology, promising research, innovative product/service delivery model, etcetera), how would your people have to approach their work and collaborate together in order to create the necessary conditions for success?
<--- Score

93. What relationships among Web customer support trends do you perceive?
<--- Score

94. To whom do you add value?
<--- Score

95. What may be the consequences for the performance of an organization if all stakeholders are not consulted regarding Web customer support?

<--- Score

96. Is it economical; do you have the time and money?
<--- Score

97. What is your question? Why?

<--- Score

98. Why do and why don't your customers like your organization?

<--- Score

99. How do you create buy-in?

<--- Score

100. How much contingency will be available in the budget?
<--- Score

101. Do you see more potential in people than they do in themselves?
<--- Score

102. Is a Web customer support breakthrough on the horizon?
<--- Score

103. What counts that you are not counting?
<--- Score

104. Are you satisfied with your current role? If not, what is missing from it?

<--- Score

105. Political -is anyone trying to undermine this project?
<--- Score

106. What are the essentials of internal Web customer support management?
<--- Score

107. Is the impact that Web customer support has shown?
<--- Score

108. If you got fired and a new hire took your place, what would she do different?
<--- Score

109. How do you know if you are successful?
<--- Score

110. Who will manage the integration of tools?
<--- Score

111. What did you miss in the interview for the worst hire you ever made?
<--- Score

112. What is something you believe that nearly no one agrees with you on?
<--- Score

113. Do you say no to customers for no reason?
<--- Score

114. What are your personal philosophies regarding

Web customer support and how do they influence
your work?
<--- Score

115. What is the funding source for this project?
<--- Score

116. Which individuals, teams or departments will be
involved in Web customer support?
<--- Score

117. If there were zero limitations, what would you do
differently?
<--- Score

**118. How will you insure seamless interoperability
of Web customer support moving forward?**
<--- Score

119. What would have to be true for the option on the
table to be the best possible choice?
<--- Score

120. Do you know who is a friend or a foe?
<--- Score

121. What does your signature ensure?
<--- Score

122. How long will it take to change?
<--- Score

123. What is the big Web customer support idea?
<--- Score

124. Will it be accepted by users?

<--- Score

125. Are the criteria for selecting recommendations stated?
<--- Score

126. If you weren't already in this business, would you enter it today? And if not, what are you going to do about it?
<--- Score

127. Think of your Web customer support project, what are the main functions?
<--- Score

128. Are you maintaining a past–present–future perspective throughout the Web customer support discussion?
<--- Score

129. What potential megatrends could make your business model obsolete?
<--- Score

130. Who, on the executive team or the board, has spoken to a customer recently?
<--- Score

131. What happens when a new employee joins the organization?
<--- Score

132. How can you negotiate Web customer support successfully with a stubborn boss, an irate client, or a deceitful coworker?
<--- Score

133. What is the craziest thing you can do?
<--- Score

134. What are the key enablers to make this Web customer support move?
<--- Score

135. How can you incorporate support to ensure safe and effective use of Web customer support into the services that you provide?
<--- Score

136. Has implementation been effective in reaching specified objectives so far?
<--- Score

137. What is the range of capabilities?
<--- Score

138. Why is Web customer support important for you now?
<--- Score

139. Are you making progress, and are you making progress as Web customer support leaders?
<--- Score

140. Why will customers want to buy your organizations products/services?
<--- Score

141. Do you have the right people on the bus?
<--- Score

142. How can you become more high-tech but still

be high touch?
<--- Score

143. How do you deal with Web customer support changes?
<--- Score

144. What happens at your organization when people fail?
<--- Score

145. Have benefits been optimized with all key stakeholders?
<--- Score

146. What is a feasible sequencing of reform initiatives over time?
<--- Score

147. Is there any reason to believe the opposite of my current belief?
<--- Score

148. What is the overall talent health of your organization as a whole at senior levels, and for each organization reporting to a member of the Senior Leadership Team?
<--- Score

149. What projects are going on in the organization today, and what resources are those projects using from the resource pools?
<--- Score

150. Marketing budgets are tighter, consumers are more skeptical, and social media has changed forever

the way we talk about Web customer support, how do you gain traction?
<--- Score

151. How do you govern and fulfill your societal responsibilities?
<--- Score

152. Is maximizing Web customer support protection the same as minimizing Web customer support loss?
<--- Score

153. What are internal and external Web customer support relations?
<--- Score

154. How will you know that the Web customer support project has been successful?
<--- Score

155. What one word do you want to own in the minds of your customers, employees, and partners?
<--- Score

156. Instead of going to current contacts for new ideas, what if you reconnected with dormant contacts--the people you used to know? If you were going reactivate a dormant tie, who would it be?
<--- Score

157. What are current Web customer support paradigms?
<--- Score

158. What new services of functionality will be implemented next with Web customer support ?
<--- Score

159. Can you maintain your growth without detracting from the factors that have contributed to your success?
<--- Score

160. In retrospect, of the projects that you pulled the plug on, what percent do you wish had been allowed to keep going, and what percent do you wish had ended earlier?
<--- Score

161. What are the short and long-term Web customer support goals?
<--- Score

162. Are new benefits received and understood?
<--- Score

163. What Web customer support skills are most important?
<--- Score

164. What is your formula for success in Web customer support ?
<--- Score

165. Who will provide the final approval of Web customer support deliverables?
<--- Score

166. Do you have past Web customer support successes?

<--- Score

167. What could happen if you do not do it?
<--- Score

168. Ask yourself: how would you do this work if you only had one staff member to do it?
<--- Score

169. What is the purpose of Web customer support in relation to the mission?
<--- Score

170. Who uses your product in ways you never expected?
<--- Score

171. What happens if you do not have enough funding?
<--- Score

172. How does Web customer support integrate with other stakeholder initiatives?
<--- Score

173. How do you maintain Web customer support's Integrity?
<--- Score

174. What are the usability implications of Web customer support actions?
<--- Score

175. Whose voice (department, ethnic group, women, older workers, etc) might you have missed hearing from in your company, and how might you amplify

this voice to create positive momentum for your business?
<--- Score

176. What should you stop doing?
<--- Score

177. What stupid rule would you most like to kill?
<--- Score

178. Are your responses positive or negative?
<--- Score

179. How do you proactively clarify deliverables and Web customer support quality expectations?
<--- Score

180. How do you accomplish your long range Web customer support goals?
<--- Score

181. What unique value proposition (UVP) do you offer?
<--- Score

182. What are the gaps in your knowledge and experience?
<--- Score

183. Can the schedule be done in the given time?
<--- Score

184. In the past year, what have you done (or could you have done) to increase the accurate perception of your company/brand as ethical and honest?

<--- Score

185. Do you think Web customer support accomplishes the goals you expect it to accomplish?
<--- Score

186. What is your competitive advantage?
<--- Score

187. How will you ensure you get what you expected?
<--- Score

188. How do you keep the momentum going?
<--- Score

189. How do you cross-sell and up-sell your Web customer support success?
<--- Score

190. How will you motivate the stakeholders with the least vested interest?
<--- Score

191. What is it like to work for you?
<--- Score

192. How important is Web customer support to the user organizations mission?
<--- Score

193. Why should people listen to you?
<--- Score

194. Do you feel that more should be done in the Web

customer support area?

<--- Score

195. Is Web customer support realistic, or are you setting yourself up for failure?

<--- Score

196. How do you stay inspired?

<--- Score

197. What have you done to protect your business from competitive encroachment?

<--- Score

198. What goals did you miss?

<--- Score

199. Are you using a design thinking approach and integrating Innovation, Web customer support Experience, and Brand Value?

<--- Score

200. Why is it important to have senior management support for a Web customer support project?

<--- Score

201. How do you ensure that implementations of Web customer support products are done in a way that ensures safety?

<--- Score

202. What is the estimated value of the project?

<--- Score

203. Is the Web customer support organization

completing tasks effectively and efficiently?
<--- Score

204. What you are going to do to affect the numbers?
<--- Score

205. Who else should you help?
<--- Score

206. Are the assumptions believable and achievable?
<--- Score

207. Which Web customer support goals are the most important?
<--- Score

208. How do you go about securing Web customer support?
<--- Score

Add up total points for this section:
_ _ _ _ _ = Total points for this section

Divided by: _ _ _ _ _ _ (number of
statements answered) = _ _ _ _ _ _
Average score for this section

Transfer your score to the Web customer
support Index at the beginning of the
Self-Assessment.

Web Customer Support and Managing Projects, Criteria for Project Managers:

1.0 Initiating Process Group: Web Customer Support

1. What were things that you need to improve?

2. Who is involved in each phase?

3. Have the stakeholders identified all individual requirements pertaining to business process?

4. Which six sigma dmaic phase focuses on why and how defects and errors occur?

5. What were things that you did well, and could improve, and how?

6. Are you certain deliverables are properly completed and meet quality standards?

7. Who supports, improves, and oversees standardized processes related to the Web Customer Support projects program?

8. How do you help others satisfy needs?

9. Information sharing?

10. The process to Manage Stakeholders is part of which process group?

11. At which cmmi level are software processes documented, standardized, and integrated into a standard to-be practiced process for your organization?

12. Are you just doing busywork to pass the time?

13. Do you understand the quality and control criteria that must be achieved for successful Web Customer Support project completion?

14. During which stage of Risk planning are risks prioritized based on probability and impact?

15. What do you need to do?

16. Were resources available as planned?

17. What are the inputs required to produce the deliverables?

18. What are the constraints?

19. What input will you be required to provide the Web Customer Support project team?

20. What areas were overlooked on this Web Customer Support project?

1.1 Project Charter: Web Customer Support

21. What outcome, in measureable terms, are you hoping to accomplish?

22. Why have you chosen the aim you have set forth?

23. What are the deliverables?

24. Why use a Web Customer Support project charter?

25. How do you manage integration?

26. What is the purpose of the Web Customer Support project?

27. How will you know that a change is an improvement?

28. Is it an improvement over existing products?

29. Are you building in-house ?

30. How high should you set your goals?

31. What ideas do you have for initial tests of change (PDSA cycles)?

32. Run it as as a startup?

33. Did your Web Customer Support project ask for this?

34. What are some examples of a business case?

35. Customer: who are you doing the Web Customer Support project for?

36. Market – identify products market, including whether it is outside of the objective: what is the purpose of the program or Web Customer Support project?

37. Who is the Web Customer Support project Manager?

38. What is the business need?

39. Are there special technology requirements?

1.2 Stakeholder Register: Web Customer Support

40. How should employers make voices heard?

41. What opportunities exist to provide communications?

42. Who are the stakeholders?

43. How much influence do they have on the Web Customer Support project?

44. Who is managing stakeholder engagement?

45. What are the major Web Customer Support project milestones requiring communications or providing communications opportunities?

46. How big is the gap?

47. Is your organization ready for change?

48. How will reports be created?

49. What is the power of the stakeholder?

50. What & Why?

51. Who wants to talk about Security?

1.3 Stakeholder Analysis Matrix: Web Customer Support

52. Is there a clear description of the scope of practice of the Web Customer Support projects educators?

53. Guiding question: who shall you involve in the making of the stakeholder map?

54. What advantages do your organizations stakeholders have?

55. Are there two or three that rise to the top, and a couple that are sliding to the bottom?

56. Philosophy and values?

57. Competitive advantages?

58. How to measure the achievement of the Outputs?

59. Which conditions out of the control of the management are crucial to contribute for the achievement of the development objective?

60. What do you Evaluate?

61. Who can contribute financial or technical resources towards the work?

62. Disadvantages of proposition?

63. Who will be responsible for managing the

outcome?

64. Who determines value?

65. Marketing - reach, distribution, awareness?

66. Management cover, succession?

67. Sustainable financial backing?

68. Are there different rules or organizational models for men and women?

69. What are the mechanisms of public and social accountability, and how can they be made better?

2.0 Planning Process Group: Web Customer Support

70. When developing the estimates for Web Customer Support project phases, you choose to add the individual estimates for the activities that comprise each phase. What type of estimation method are you using?

71. In which Web Customer Support project management process group is the detailed Web Customer Support project budget created?

72. In what way has the Web Customer Support project come up with innovative measures for problem-solving?

73. If task x starts two days late, what is the effect on the Web Customer Support project end date?

74. If action is called for, what form should it take?

75. To what extent have the target population and participants made the activities own, taking an active role in it?

76. If you are late, will anybody notice?

77. Professionals want to know what is expected from them; what are the deliverables?

78. What are the different approaches to building the WBS?

79. If a task is partitionable, is this a sufficient condition to reduce the Web Customer Support project duration?

80. Product breakdown structure (pbs): what is the Web Customer Support project result or product, and how should it look like, what are its parts?

81. Who are the Web Customer Support project stakeholders?

82. Explanation: is what the Web Customer Support project intents to solve a hard question?

83. Did the program design/ implementation strategy adequately address the planning stage necessary to set up structures, hire staff etc.?

84. Mitigate. what will you do to minimize the impact should a risk event occur?

85. To what extent has a PMO contributed to raising the quality of the design of the Web Customer Support project?

86. How well did the chosen processes fit the needs of the Web Customer Support project?

87. What should you do next?

88. Is the Web Customer Support project supported by national and/or local organizations?

2.1 Project Management Plan: Web Customer Support

89. Do there need to be organizational changes?

90. How do you organize the costs in the Web Customer Support project management plan?

91. Are calculations and results of analyzes essentially correct?

92. If the Web Customer Support project is complex or scope is specialized, do you have appropriate and/or qualified staff available to perform the tasks?

93. When is a Web Customer Support project management plan created?

94. Are the proposed Web Customer Support project purposes different than a previously authorized Web Customer Support project?

95. Are there any windfall benefits that would accrue to the Web Customer Support project sponsor or other parties?

96. Are comparable cost estimates used for comparing, screening and selecting alternative plans, and has a reasonable cost estimate been developed for the recommended plan?

97. Is there anything you would now do differently on your Web Customer Support project based on past

experience?

98. Did the planning effort collaborate to develop solutions that integrate expertise, policies, programs, and Web Customer Support projects across entities?

99. What is risk management?

100. Is the budget realistic?

101. What does management expect of PMs?

102. Who is the Web Customer Support project Manager?

103. Are there non-structural buyout or relocation recommendations?

104. What are the assigned resources?

105. What are the known stakeholder requirements?

106. Is mitigation authorized or recommended?

2.2 Scope Management Plan: Web Customer Support

107. Quality standards - are controls in place to ensure that the work was not only completed and also completed to meet specific standards?

108. Are you spending the right amount of money for specific tasks?

109. What is your organizations history in doing similar activities?

110. Are internal Web Customer Support project status meetings held at reasonable intervals?

111. The greatest degree of uncertainty is encountered during which phase of the Web Customer Support project life cycle?

112. Pop quiz – what changed on Web Customer Support project scope statement input?

113. Are risk triggers captured?

114. What is the relative power of the Web Customer Support project manager?

115. What does the critical path really mean?

116. For which criterion is it tolerable not to meet the original parameters?

117. Is there an approved case?

118. What is the most common tool for helping define the detail?

119. Has a capability assessment been conducted?

120. Were Web Customer Support project team members involved in the development of activity & task decomposition?

121. Are you doing what you have set out to do?

122. Staffing Requirements?

123. Is it standard practice to formally commit stakeholders to the Web Customer Support project via agreements?

124. Function of the configuration control board?

125. Are there procedures in place to effectively manage interdependencies with other Web Customer Support projects, systems, Vendors and your organizations work effort?

126. Are there any scope changes proposed for the previously authorized Web Customer Support project?

2.3 Requirements Management Plan: Web Customer Support

127. What are you trying to do?

128. Is the user satisfied?

129. Will you use tracing to help understand the impact of a change in requirements?

130. Who will initially review the Web Customer Support project work or products to ensure it meets the applicable acceptance criteria?

131. What went right?

132. Did you avoid subjective, flowery or non-specific statements?

133. Will you have access to stakeholders when you need them?

134. Who has the authority to reject Web Customer Support project requirements?

135. Do you understand the role that each stakeholder will play in the requirements process?

136. Why manage requirements?

137. In case of software development; Should you have a test for each code module?

138. Do you have an appropriate arrangement for meetings?

139. Is it new or replacing an existing business system or process?

140. What is a problem?

141. How will the requirements become prioritized?

142. How will requirements be managed?

143. How will unresolved questions be handled once approval has been obtained?

144. Is any organizational data being used or stored?

145. How will the information be distributed?

146. Who will do the reporting and to whom will reports be delivered?

2.4 Requirements Documentation: Web Customer Support

147. How will the proposed Web Customer Support project help?

148. If applicable; are there issues linked with the fact that this is an offshore Web Customer Support project?

149. Completeness. are all functions required by the customer included?

150. Are there legal issues?

151. Where do you define what is a customer, what are the attributes of customer?

152. What images does it conjure?

153. Verifiability. can the requirements be checked?

154. What are the potential disadvantages/ advantages?

155. How do you get the user to tell you what they want?

156. What will be the integration problems?

157. Basic work/business process; high-level, what is being touched?

158. How does what is being described meet the business need?

159. Can the requirements be checked?

160. What are current process problems?

161. What is the risk associated with the technology?

162. Are there any requirements conflicts?

163. Has requirements gathering uncovered information that would necessitate changes?

164. What marketing channels do you want to use: e-mail, letter or sms?

165. Do technical resources exist?

166. Is your business case still valid?

2.5 Requirements Traceability Matrix: Web Customer Support

167. Describe the process for approving requirements so they can be added to the traceability matrix and Web Customer Support project work can be performed. Will the Web Customer Support project requirements become approved in writing?

168. How small is small enough?

169. Why do you manage scope?

170. How do you manage scope?

171. What are the chronologies, contingencies, consequences, criteria?

172. Will you use a Requirements Traceability Matrix?

173. What percentage of Web Customer Support projects are producing traceability matrices between requirements and other work products?

174. How will it affect the stakeholders personally in career?

175. Do you have a clear understanding of all subcontracts in place?

176. What is the WBS?

177. Why use a WBS?

178. Is there a requirements traceability process in place?

2.6 Project Scope Statement: Web Customer Support

179. Is this process communicated to the customer and team members?

180. If there are vendors, have they signed off on the Web Customer Support project Plan?

181. Were key Web Customer Support project stakeholders brought into the Web Customer Support project Plan?

182. Are there adequate Web Customer Support project control systems?

183. Are there completion/verification criteria defined for each task producing an output?

184. What actions will be taken to mitigate the risk?

185. What are the possible consequences should a risk come to occur?

186. Elements of scope management that deal with concept development ?

187. Web Customer Support project lead, team lead, solution architect?

188. Will tasks be marked complete only after QA has been successfully completed?

189. Did your Web Customer Support project ask for this?

190. Elements that deal with providing the detail?

191. Is the plan for your organization of the Web Customer Support project resources adequate?

192. Is there a baseline plan against which to measure progress?

193. Is your organization structure appropriate for the Web Customer Support projects size and complexity?

194. If you were to write a list of what should not be included in the scope statement, what are the things that you would recommend be described as out-of-scope?

195. Has the Web Customer Support project scope statement been reviewed as part of the baseline process?

196. Once its defined, what is the stability of the Web Customer Support project scope?

197. Will the Web Customer Support project risks be managed according to the Web Customer Support projects risk management process?

198. Will an issue form be in use?

2.7 Assumption and Constraint Log: Web Customer Support

199. How many Web Customer Support project staff does this specific process affect?

200. Do documented requirements exist for all critical components and areas, including technical, business, interfaces, performance, security and conversion requirements?

201. Is the definition of the Web Customer Support project scope clear; what needs to be accomplished?

202. Is staff trained on the software technologies that are being used on the Web Customer Support project?

203. Should factors be unpredictable over time?

204. If it is out of compliance, should the process be amended or should the Plan be amended?

205. Are there processes in place to ensure that all the terms and code concepts have been documented consistently?

206. Are you meeting your customers expectations consistently?

207. Do you know what your customers expectations are regarding this process?

208. Does a documented Web Customer Support project organizational policy & plan (i.e. governance model) exist?

209. What do you log?

210. Does the document/deliverable meet all requirements (for example, statement of work) specific to this deliverable?

211. Are processes for release management of new development from coding and unit testing, to integration testing, to training, and production defined and followed?

212. What do you audit?

213. Do the requirements meet the standards of correctness, completeness, consistency, accuracy, and readability?

214. Can you perform this task or activity in a more effective manner?

215. Are there processes in place to ensure internal consistency between the source code components?

216. Has a Web Customer Support project Communications Plan been developed?

217. Are there ways to reduce the time it takes to get something approved?

218. Does the plan conform to standards?

2.8 Work Breakdown Structure: Web Customer Support

219. What has to be done?

220. When do you stop?

221. Who has to do it?

222. When would you develop a Work Breakdown Structure?

223. Why is it useful?

224. Where does it take place?

225. Do you need another level?

226. How big is a work-package?

227. Is it a change in scope?

228. Is it still viable?

229. How many levels?

230. What is the probability that the Web Customer Support project duration will exceed xx weeks?

231. Is the work breakdown structure (wbs) defined and is the scope of the Web Customer Support project clear with assigned deliverable owners?

232. What is the probability of completing the Web Customer Support project in less that xx days?

233. How far down?

234. Can you make it?

235. When does it have to be done?

236. How much detail?

2.9 WBS Dictionary: Web Customer Support

237. The already stated responsible for overhead performance control of related costs?

238. What should you drop in order to add something new?

239. Are budgets or values assigned to work packages and planning packages in terms of dollars, hours, or other measurable units?

240. Identify potential or actual budget-based and time-based schedule variances?

241. Are the procedures for identifying indirect costs to incurring organizations, indirect cost pools, and allocating the costs from the pools to the contracts formally documented?

242. Does the contractors system identify work accomplishment against the schedule plan?

243. What went wrong?

244. The wbs is developed as part of a joint planning session. and how do you know that youhave done this right?

245. Are data being used by managers in an effective manner to ascertain Web Customer Support project or functional status, to identify reasons or significant

variance, and to initiate appropriate corrective action?

246. Time-phased control account budgets?

247. Are overhead budgets and costs being handled according to the disclosure statement when applicable, or otherwise properly classified (for example, engineering overhead, IR&D)?

248. Identify potential or actual overruns and underruns?

249. What is wrong with this Web Customer Support project?

250. Are all affected work authorizations, budgeting, and scheduling documents amended to properly reflect the effects of authorized changes?

251. Are the latest revised estimates of costs at completion compared with the established budgets at appropriate levels and causes of variances identified?

252. Does the contractor use objective results, design reviews and tests to trace schedule performance?

253. Contractor financial periods; for example, annual?

254. Does the scheduling system identify in a timely manner the status of work?

255. Are indirect costs accumulated for comparison with the corresponding budgets?

2.10 Schedule Management Plan: Web Customer Support

256. Are staff skills known and available for each task?

257. Is Web Customer Support project status reviewed with the steering and executive teams at appropriate intervals?

258. Are the payment terms being followed?

259. What date will the task finish?

260. Are the constraints or deadlines associated with the task accurate?

261. Are post milestone Web Customer Support project reviews (PMPR) conducted with your organization at least once a year?

262. Has your organization readiness assessment been conducted?

263. Is a process for scheduling and reporting defined, including forms and formats?

264. Have adequate resources been provided by management to ensure Web Customer Support project success?

265. List all schedule constraints here. Must the Web Customer Support project be complete by a specified date?

266. Is it standard practice to formally commit stakeholders to the Web Customer Support project via agreements?

267. Are estimating assumptions and constraints captured?

268. Is a payment system in place with proper reviews and approvals?

269. Can additional resources be added to subsequent tasks to reduce the durations of the already stated tasks?

270. Are cause and effect determined for risks when they occur?

271. Have the key elements of a coherent Web Customer Support project management strategy been established?

272. Are trade-offs between accepting the risk and mitigating the risk identified?

273. Are Web Customer Support project team members involved in detailed estimating and scheduling?

274. Is there a Steering Committee in place?

275. Is an industry recognized mechanized support tool(s) being used for Web Customer Support project scheduling & tracking?

2.11 Activity List: Web Customer Support

276. How should ongoing costs be monitored to try to keep the Web Customer Support project within budget?

277. What is the LF and LS for each activity?

278. What did not go as well?

279. How detailed should a Web Customer Support project get?

280. In what sequence?

281. For other activities, how much delay can be tolerated?

282. When will the work be performed?

283. Who will perform the work?

284. When do the individual activities need to start and finish?

285. What are the critical bottleneck activities?

286. Is infrastructure setup part of your Web Customer Support project?

287. What is the probability the Web Customer Support project can be completed in xx weeks?

288. Is there anything planned that does not need to be here?

289. What went well?

290. How can the Web Customer Support project be displayed graphically to better visualize the activities?

291. What are you counting on?

292. Where will it be performed?

2.12 Activity Attributes: Web Customer Support

293. Activity: what is In the Bag?

294. Which method produces the more accurate cost assignment?

295. Does your organization of the data change its meaning?

296. How many resources do you need to complete the work scope within a limit of X number of days?

297. Is there a trend during the year?

298. Can more resources be added?

299. Do you feel very comfortable with your prediction?

300. What activity do you think you should spend the most time on?

301. Time for overtime?

302. What is missing?

303. Activity: fair or not fair?

304. Have constraints been applied to the start and finish milestones for the phases?

305. What is the general pattern here?

306. Are the required resources available or need to be acquired?

307. How difficult will it be to do specific activities on this Web Customer Support project?

308. How difficult will it be to complete specific activities on this Web Customer Support project?

309. What conclusions/generalizations can you draw from this?

310. How do you manage time?

2.13 Milestone List: Web Customer Support

311. Gaps in capabilities?

312. How will the milestone be verified?

313. Can you derive how soon can the whole Web Customer Support project finish?

314. Usps (unique selling points)?

315. Describe the industry you are in and the market growth opportunities. What is the market for your technology, product or service?

316. Global influences?

317. How soon can the activity start?

318. Legislative effects?

319. Continuity, supply chain robustness?

320. Milestone pages should display the UserID of the person who added the milestone. Does a report or query exist that provides this audit information?

321. What would happen if a delivery of material was one week late?

322. How will you get the word out to customers?

323. How late can the activity start?

324. New USPs?

325. Describe the concept of the technology, product or service that will be or has been developed. How will it be used?

326. Which path is the critical path?

327. Loss of key staff?

2.14 Network Diagram: Web Customer Support

328. How difficult will it be to do specific activities on this Web Customer Support project?

329. If x is long, what would be the completion time if you break x into two parallel parts of y weeks and z weeks?

330. If a current contract exists, can you provide the vendor name, contract start, and contract expiration date?

331. What are the Major Administrative Issues?

332. What activity must be completed immediately before this activity can start?

333. What must be completed before an activity can be started?

334. Can you calculate the confidence level?

335. What job or jobs could run concurrently?

336. Why must you schedule milestones, such as reviews, throughout the Web Customer Support project?

337. Where do schedules come from?

338. Are the gantt chart and/or network diagram

updated periodically and used to assess the overall Web Customer Support project timetable?

339. Which type of network diagram allows you to depict four types of dependencies?

340. What activities must follow this activity?

341. What is the lowest cost to complete this Web Customer Support project in xx weeks?

342. What can be done concurrently?

343. Are the required resources available?

344. Where do you schedule uncertainty time?

345. What job or jobs follow it?

346. Will crashing x weeks return more in benefits than it costs?

347. What controls the start and finish of a job?

2.15 Activity Resource Requirements: Web Customer Support

348. Organizational Applicability?

349. Do you use tools like decomposition and rolling-wave planning to produce the activity list and other outputs?

350. Anything else?

351. Why do you do that?

352. Other support in specific areas?

353. What is the Work Plan Standard?

354. What are constraints that you might find during the Human Resource Planning process?

355. Are there unresolved issues that need to be addressed?

356. How many signatures do you require on a check and does this match what is in your policy and procedures?

357. When does monitoring begin?

358. How do you handle petty cash?

359. Which logical relationship does the PDM use most often?

2.16 Resource Breakdown Structure: Web Customer Support

360. Who is allowed to see what data about which resources?

361. Is predictive resource analysis being done?

362. The list could probably go on, but, the thing that you would most like to know is, How long & How much?

363. Who will be used as a Web Customer Support project team member?

364. Who will use the system?

365. Who needs what information?

366. Who delivers the information?

367. How difficult will it be to do specific activities on this Web Customer Support project?

368. What is Web Customer Support project communication management?

369. When do they need the information?

370. What is the difference between % Complete and % work?

371. Goals for the Web Customer Support project.

What is each stakeholders desired outcome for the Web Customer Support project?

372. Which resources should be in the resource pool?

373. Why is this important?

2.17 Activity Duration Estimates: Web Customer Support

374. What are the largest companies that provide information technology outsourcing services?

375. Is the Web Customer Support project performing better or worse than planned?

376. What is involved in the solicitation process?

377. Are reward and recognition systems defined to promote or reinforce desired behavior?

378. If you plan to take the PMP exam soon, what should you do to prepare?

379. Briefly summarize the work done by Maslow, Herzberg, McClellan, McGregor, Ouchi, Thamhain and Wilemon, and Covey. How do theories relate to Web Customer Support project management?

380. Are activity duration estimates documented?

381. Web Customer Support project manager has received activity duration estimates from his team. Which does one need in order to complete schedule development?

382. Will additional funds be needed for hardware or software?

383. What is the duration of the critical path for this

Web Customer Support project?

384. What is done after activity duration estimation?

385. Are steps identified by which Web Customer Support project documents may be changed?

386. Are the causes of all variances identified?

387. Who will promote it?

388. Will new hardware or software be required for servers or client machines?

389. Does a process exist for approving or rejecting changes?

390. What do you think the real problem was in this case?

391. Which best describes how this affects the Web Customer Support project?

2.18 Duration Estimating Worksheet: Web Customer Support

392. When, then?

393. Define the work as completely as possible. What work will be included in the Web Customer Support project?

394. Value pocket identification & quantification what are value pockets?

395. Does the Web Customer Support project provide innovative ways for stakeholders to overcome obstacles or deliver better outcomes?

396. Why estimate costs?

397. What info is needed?

398. What utility impacts are there?

399. Small or large Web Customer Support project?

400. Do any colleagues have experience with your organization and/or RFPs?

401. Will the Web Customer Support project collaborate with the local community and leverage resources?

402. Can the Web Customer Support project be constructed as planned?

403. What is next?

404. What is the total time required to complete the Web Customer Support project if no delays occur?

405. When does your organization expect to be able to complete it?

406. Is the Web Customer Support project responsive to community need?

407. Is this operation cost effective?

408. What is cost and Web Customer Support project cost management?

2.19 Project Schedule: Web Customer Support

409. What is risk?

410. Why do you think schedule issues often cause the most conflicts on Web Customer Support projects?

411. How do you use schedules?

412. How does a Web Customer Support project get to be a year late ?

413. Was the Web Customer Support project schedule reviewed by all stakeholders and formally accepted?

414. How do you manage Web Customer Support project Risk?

415. What is the difference?

416. What is Web Customer Support project management?

417. How can you shorten the schedule?

418. Are the original Web Customer Support project schedule and budget realistic?

419. Did the Web Customer Support project come in on schedule?

420. Your best shot for providing estimations how

complex/how much work does the activity require?

421. What documents, if any, will the subcontractor provide (eg Web Customer Support project schedule, quality plan etc)?

422. Understand the constraints used in preparing the schedule. Are activities connected because logic dictates the order in which others occur?

423. Are all remaining durations correct?

424. Should you include sub-activities?

425. How can you address that situation?

426. Is the structure for tracking the Web Customer Support project schedule well defined and assigned to a specific individual?

2.20 Cost Management Plan: Web Customer Support

427. Are the schedule estimates reasonable given the Web Customer Support project?

428. Are key risk mitigation strategies added to the Web Customer Support project schedule?

429. Is Web Customer Support project work proceeding in accordance with the original Web Customer Support project schedule?

430. Designated small business reserve?

431. Was the Web Customer Support project schedule reviewed by all stakeholders and formally accepted?

432. Are mitigation strategies identified?

433. Is there an on-going process in place to monitor Web Customer Support project risks?

434. How do you manage cost?

435. Responsibilities – what is the split of responsibilities between the owner and contractors?

436. Have key stakeholders been identified?

437. Does the Web Customer Support project have a Quality Culture?

438. Planning and scheduling responsibilities – How will the responsibilities for planning and scheduling be allocated?

439. Contracting method – what contracting method is to be used for the contracts?

440. Is there an issues management plan in place?

441. Are status reports received per the Web Customer Support project Plan?

442. Are procurement deliverables arriving on time and to specification?

443. Progress measurement and control – How will the Web Customer Support project measure and control progress?

444. Outside experts?

445. Does the schedule include Web Customer Support project management time and change request analysis time?

2.21 Activity Cost Estimates: Web Customer Support

446. How quickly can the task be done with the skills available?

447. What communication items need improvement?

448. Who determines when the contractor is paid?

449. Are cost subtotals needed?

450. Specific - is the objective clear in terms of what, how, when, and where the situation will be changed?

451. Were decisions made in a timely manner?

452. How Award?

453. Eac -estimate at completion, what is the total job expected to cost?

454. Can you delete activities or make them inactive?

455. Are data needed on characteristics of care?

456. Were you satisfied with the work?

457. Why do you manage cost?

458. Is costing method consistent with study goals?

459. Will you use any tools, such as Web Customer

Support project management software, to assist in capturing Earned Value metrics?

460. How do you allocate indirect costs to activities?

461. What are the audit requirements?

462. What happens if you cannot produce the documentation for the single audit?

463. How many activities should you have?

464. What defines a successful Web Customer Support project?

2.22 Cost Estimating Worksheet: Web Customer Support

465. Does the Web Customer Support project provide innovative ways for stakeholders to overcome obstacles or deliver better outcomes?

466. What costs are to be estimated?

467. How will the results be shared and to whom?

468. Is it feasible to establish a control group arrangement?

469. Ask: are others positioned to know, are others credible, and will others cooperate?

470. Is the Web Customer Support project responsive to community need?

471. What is the estimated labor cost today based upon this information?

472. What is the purpose of estimating?

473. Will the Web Customer Support project collaborate with the local community and leverage resources?

474. Identify the timeframe necessary to monitor progress and collect data to determine how the selected measure has changed?

475. What additional Web Customer Support project(s) could be initiated as a result of this Web Customer Support project?

476. What can be included?

477. Can a trend be established from historical performance data on the selected measure and are the criteria for using trend analysis or forecasting methods met?

478. Who is best positioned to know and assist in identifying corresponding factors?

479. What will others want?

480. What happens to any remaining funds not used?

2.23 Cost Baseline: Web Customer Support

481. Have you identified skills that are missing from your team?

482. What is the consequence?

483. What is the most important thing to do next to make your Web Customer Support project successful?

484. Who will use corresponding metrics ?

485. Are you meeting with your team regularly?

486. Does the suggested change request seem to represent a necessary enhancement to the product?

487. Have all approved changes to the schedule baseline been identified and impact on the Web Customer Support project documented?

488. What would the life cycle costs be?

489. What strengths do you have?

490. What weaknesses do you have?

491. On budget?

492. Is there anything you need from upper management in order to be successful?

493. Have the resources used by the Web Customer Support project been reassigned to other units or Web Customer Support projects?

494. When should cost estimates be developed?

495. Is request in line with priorities?

496. How fast?

497. Has operations management formally accepted responsibility for operating and maintaining the product(s) or service(s) delivered by the Web Customer Support project?

498. Have all the product or service deliverables been accepted by the customer?

499. What can go wrong?

2.24 Quality Management Plan: Web Customer Support

500. How is staff trained in procedures?

501. How does your organization manage work to promote cooperation, individual initiative, innovation, flexibility, communications, and knowledge/skill sharing across work units?

502. Checking the completeness and appropriateness of the sampling and testing. Were the right locations/ samples tested for the right parameters?

503. Who is approving the QAPP?

504. How are corresponding standards measured?

505. How does your organization make it easy for customers to seek assistance or complain?

506. How do you ensure that protocols are up to date?

507. How are changes to procedures made?

508. Can it be done better?

509. How are people conducting sampling trained?

510. Are qmps good forever?

511. Modifications to the requirements?

512. How are senior leaders, employees, and your organization involved in supporting the community?

513. Who gets results of work?

514. Are requirements management tracking tools and procedures in place?

515. What type of in-house testing do you conduct?

516. How do you ensure that your sampling methods and procedures meet your data quality objectives?

517. How does your organization maintain a safe and healthy work environment?

518. What process do you use to minimize errors, defects, and rework?

519. Who is responsible?

2.25 Quality Metrics: Web Customer Support

520. Where did complaints, returns and warranty claims come from?

521. How exactly do you define when differences exist?

522. Have alternatives been defined in the event that failure occurs?

523. How do you calculate corresponding metrics?

524. What are your organizations expectations for its quality Web Customer Support project?

525. Is the reporting frequency appropriate?

526. Did evaluation start on time?

527. Are documents on hand to provide explanations of privacy and confidentiality?

528. Is there alignment within your organization on definitions?

529. Is quality culture a competitive advantage?

530. What can manufacturing professionals do to ensure quality is seen as an integral part of the entire product lifecycle?

531. What if the biggest risk to your business were the already stated people who do not complain?

532. How effective are your security tests?

533. How should customers provide input?

534. How is it being measured?

535. What are you trying to accomplish?

536. The metrics–what is being considered?

537. Are there already quality metrics available that detect nonlinear embeddings and trends similar to the users perception?

538. Has trace of defects been initiated?

539. Have risk areas been identified?

2.26 Process Improvement Plan: Web Customer Support

540. Are you meeting the quality standards?

541. Management commitment at all levels?

542. What is quality and how will you ensure it?

543. Have the supporting tools been developed or acquired?

544. What is the test-cycle concept?

545. If a process improvement framework is being used, which elements will help the problems and goals listed?

546. To elicit goal statements, do you ask a question such as, What do you want to achieve?

547. Who should prepare the process improvement action plan?

548. Does your process ensure quality?

549. What personnel are the champions for the initiative?

550. Everyone agrees on what process improvement is, right?

551. Have storage and access mechanisms and

procedures been determined?

552. Are you making progress on the goals?

553. What lessons have you learned so far?

554. Where are you now?

555. Does explicit definition of the measures exist?

556. Are there forms and procedures to collect and record the data?

557. The motive is determined by asking, Why do you want to achieve this goal?

558. Are you following the quality standards?

2.27 Responsibility Assignment Matrix: Web Customer Support

559. Changes in the overhead pool and/or organization structures?

560. Are people encouraged to bring up issues?

561. Detailed schedules which support control account and work package start and completion dates/events?

562. Is accountability placed at the lowest-possible level within the Web Customer Support project so that decisions can be made at that level?

563. Incurrence of actual indirect costs in excess of budgets, by element of expense?

564. Who is going to do that work?

565. What can you do to improve productivity?

566. Where does all this information come from?

567. Do work packages consist of discrete tasks which are adequately described?

568. Budgeted cost for work scheduled?

569. What happens when others get pulled for higher priority Web Customer Support projects?

570. Most people let you know when others re too busy, and are others really too busy?

571. Is work progressively subdivided into detailed work packages as requirements are defined?

572. What are some important Web Customer Support project communications management tools?

573. How many hours by each staff member/rate?

574. Evaluate the performance of operating organizations?

575. Is budgeted cost for work performed calculated in a manner consistent with the way work is planned?

576. How do you manage remotely to staff in other Divisions?

577. Are work packages assigned to performing organizations?

2.28 Roles and Responsibilities: Web Customer Support

578. Does your vision/mission support a culture of quality data?

579. To decide whether to use a quality measurement, ask how will you know when it is achieved?

580. Are the quality assurance functions and related roles and responsibilities clearly defined?

581. Who is involved?

582. What is working well?

583. Who: who is involved?

584. Is feedback clearly communicated and non-judgmental?

585. Once the responsibilities are defined for the Web Customer Support project, have the deliverables, roles and responsibilities been clearly communicated to every participant?

586. Be specific; avoid generalities. Thank you and great work alone are insufficient. What exactly do you appreciate and why?

587. Are your budgets supportive of a culture of quality data?

588. Was the expectation clearly communicated?

589. What areas would you highlight for changes or improvements?

590. Attainable / achievable: the goal is attainable; can you actually accomplish the goal?

591. Are governance roles and responsibilities documented?

592. Do you take the time to clearly define roles and responsibilities on Web Customer Support project tasks?

593. Have you ever been a part of this team?

594. What should you do now to prepare yourself for a promotion, increased responsibilities or a different job?

595. Concern: where are you limited or have no authority, where you can not influence?

596. Who is responsible for each task?

2.29 Human Resource Management Plan: Web Customer Support

597. Has the business need been clearly defined?

598. Has the Web Customer Support project scope been baselined?

599. Are all key components of a Quality Assurance Plan present?

600. What are the Staffing Requirements?

601. Are cause and effect determined for risks when others occur?

602. Has a provision been made to reassess Web Customer Support project risks at various Web Customer Support project stages?

603. Is this Web Customer Support project carried out in partnership with other groups/organizations?

604. Were Web Customer Support project team members involved in the development of activity & task decomposition?

605. Is there a formal set of procedures supporting Stakeholder Management?

606. Is there a formal set of procedures supporting Issues Management?

607. Are risk oriented checklists used during risk identification?

608. Is the current culture aligned with the vision, mission, and values of the department?

609. Does the schedule include Web Customer Support project management time and change request analysis time?

610. Are Web Customer Support project team members involved in detailed estimating and scheduling?

611. What commitments have been made?

612. Do people have the competencies to meet the strategic objectives?

2.30 Communications Management Plan: Web Customer Support

613. Are you constantly rushing from meeting to meeting?

614. Which team member will work with each stakeholder?

615. How did the term stakeholder originate?

616. Why do you manage communications?

617. What steps can you take for a positive relationship?

618. How is this initiative related to other portfolios, programs, or Web Customer Support projects?

619. Who have you worked with in past, similar initiatives?

620. Will messages be directly related to the release strategy or phases of the Web Customer Support project?

621. Who will use or be affected by the result of a Web Customer Support project?

622. Who needs to know and how much?

623. What is the stakeholders level of authority?

624. How much time does it take to do it?

625. What are the interrelationships?

626. What approaches to you feel are the best ones to use?

627. Do you then often overlook a key stakeholder or stakeholder group?

628. What is the political influence?

629. Why manage stakeholders?

630. What approaches do you use?

2.31 Risk Management Plan: Web Customer Support

631. Risk may be made during which step of risk management?

632. Premium on reliability of product?

633. Was an original risk assessment/risk management plan completed?

634. How quickly does this item need to be resolved?

635. What are the cost, schedule and resource impacts of avoiding the risk?

636. Can the Web Customer Support project proceed without assuming the risk?

637. Are certain activities taking a long time to complete?

638. What are the chances the risk event will occur?

639. What is the cost to the Web Customer Support project if it does occur?

640. Are the reports useful and easy to read?

641. Does the software engineering team have the right mix of skills?

642. Is there anything you would now do differently

on your Web Customer Support project based on this experience?

643. How is risk response planning performed?

644. Are requirements fully understood by the software engineering team and customers?

645. Which risks should get the attention?

646. What other risks are created by choosing an avoidance strategy?

647. Are tool mentors available?

648. Could others have been better mitigated?

649. Are the metrics meaningful and useful?

650. What did not work so well?

2.32 Risk Register: Web Customer Support

651. Methodology: how will risk management be performed on this Web Customer Support project?

652. When would you develop a risk register?

653. Who needs to know about this?

654. What should you do now?

655. Amongst the action plans and recommendations that you have to introduce are there some that could stop or delay the overall program?

656. Manageability – have mitigations to the risk been identified?

657. Preventative actions - planned actions to reduce the likelihood a risk will occur and/or reduce the seriousness should it occur. What should you do now?

658. What are the assumptions and current status that support the assessment of the risk?

659. What is your current and future risk profile?

660. Are implemented controls working as others should?

661. Risk documentation: what reporting formats and processes will be used for risk management activities?

662. What could prevent you delivering on the strategic program objectives and what is being done to mitigate corresponding issues?

663. Do you require further engagement?

664. Risk categories: what are the main categories of risks that should be addressed on this Web Customer Support project?

665. When is it going to be done?

666. Assume the event happens, what is the Most Likely impact?

667. How often will the Risk Management Plan and Risk Register be formally reviewed, and by whom?

668. Recovery actions - planned actions taken once a risk has occurred to allow you to move on. What should you do after?

669. What can be done about it?

2.33 Probability and Impact Assessment: Web Customer Support

670. How carefully have the potential competitors been identified?

671. What are your data sources?

672. Have customers been involved fully in the definition of requirements?

673. Do you use any methods to analyze risks?

674. Who will be responsible for a slippage?

675. Are the risk data complete?

676. Have top software and customer managers formally committed to support the Web Customer Support project?

677. Is security a central objective?

678. What risks does your organization have if the Web Customer Support projects fail to meet deadline?

679. What should be the external organizations responsibility vis-à-vis total stake in the Web Customer Support project?

680. Are the best people available?

681. Who should be responsible for the monitoring

and tracking of the indicators youhave identified?

682. Are staff committed for the duration of the Web Customer Support project?

683. Which role do you have in the Web Customer Support project?

684. What is the likelihood of a breakthrough?

685. How solid is the Web Customer Support projection of competitive reaction?

686. Is the process supported by tools?

687. Risks should be identified during which phase of Web Customer Support project management life cycle?

688. Are trained personnel, including supervisors and Web Customer Support project managers, available to handle such a large Web Customer Support project?

689. Are team members trained in the use of the tools?

2.34 Probability and Impact Matrix: Web Customer Support

690. Are enough people available?

691. Are tools for analysis and design available?

692. Do the requirements require the creation of new algorithms?

693. Which of the risk factors can be avoided altogether?

694. If you can not fix it, how do you do it differently?

695. Are staff committed for the duration of the Web Customer Support project?

696. Do requirements demand the use of new analysis, design, or testing methods?

697. How solid is the Web Customer Support projection of competitive reaction?

698. Are the risk data timely and relevant?

699. What are the uncertainties associated with the technology selected for the Web Customer Support project?

700. What lifestyle shifts might occur in society?

701. Which should be probably done NEXT?

702. Do you have a consistent repeatable process that is actually used?

703. Were there any Web Customer Support projects similar to this one in existence?

704. How do you define a risk?

705. What is the risk appetite?

706. What are the methods to deal with risks?

2.35 Risk Data Sheet: Web Customer Support

707. What are the main opportunities available to you that you should grab while you can?

708. What do people affected think about the need for, and practicality of preventive measures?

709. What if client refuses?

710. How can it happen?

711. Potential for recurrence?

712. Has the most cost-effective solution been chosen?

713. If it happens, what are the consequences?

714. How reliable is the data source?

715. How can hazards be reduced?

716. Type of risk identified?

717. What do you know?

718. Whom do you serve (customers)?

719. What is the environment within which you operate (social trends, economic, community values, broad based participation, national directions etc.)?

720. What are you weak at and therefore need to do better?

721. What are you trying to achieve (Objectives)?

722. Risk of what?

723. What is the likelihood of it happening?

724. During work activities could hazards exist?

725. What are your core values?

2.36 Procurement Management Plan: Web Customer Support

726. Has Web Customer Support project success criteria been defined?

727. Was your organizations estimating methodology being used and followed?

728. Are written status reports provided on a designated frequent basis?

729. Financial capacity; does the seller have, or can the seller reasonably be expected to obtain, the financial resources needed?

730. Are milestone deliverables effectively tracked and compared to Web Customer Support project plan?

731. Are target dates established for each milestone deliverable?

732. Is it standard practice to formally commit stakeholders to the Web Customer Support project via agreements?

733. Has the Web Customer Support project manager been identified?

734. Are Web Customer Support project team members committed fulltime?

735. Web Customer Support project Objectives?

736. Have process improvement efforts been completed before requirements efforts begin?

737. What areas are overlooked on this Web Customer Support project?

738. Does the business case include how the Web Customer Support project aligns with your organizations strategic goals & objectives?

739. Are the appropriate IT resources adequate to meet planned commitments?

740. Is the Web Customer Support project schedule available for all Web Customer Support project team members to review?

741. What areas does the group agree are the biggest success on the Web Customer Support project?

742. Are post milestone Web Customer Support project reviews (PMPR) conducted with your organization at least once a year?

743. Are Web Customer Support project leaders committed to this Web Customer Support project full time?

744. Is Web Customer Support project work proceeding in accordance with the original Web Customer Support project schedule?

2.37 Source Selection Criteria: Web Customer Support

745. How will you evaluate offerors proposals?

746. Do proposed hours support content and schedule?

747. What are the steps in performing a cost/tech tradeoff?

748. Is this a cost contract?

749. What common questions or problems are associated with debriefings?

750. Do you ensure you evaluate what you asked for, not what you want to see or expect to see?

751. Are responses to considerations adequate?

752. Has all proposal data been loaded?

753. How can business terms and conditions be improved to yield more effective price competition?

754. Which contract type places the most risk on the seller?

755. What are the requirements for publicizing a RFP?

756. In which phase of the acquisition process cycle does source qualifications reside?

757. What risks were identified in the proposals?

758. Who is entitled to a debriefing?

759. Will the technical evaluation factor unnecessarily force the acquisition into a higher-priced market segment?

760. What should clarifications include?

761. How long will it take for the purchase cost to be the same as the lease cost?

762. Are evaluators ready to begin this task?

763. When is it appropriate to conduct a preproposal conference?

764. Is there collaboration among your evaluators?

2.38 Stakeholder Management Plan: Web Customer Support

765. Are Web Customer Support project team members involved in detailed estimating and scheduling?

766. Is there an onboarding process in place?

767. What preventative action can be taken to reduce the likelihood a risk will be realised?

768. Has the scope management document been updated and distributed to help prevent scope creep?

769. Are the Web Customer Support project team members located locally to the users/stakeholders?

770. When would you develop a Web Customer Support project Business Plan?

771. How are new requirements or changes to requirements identified?

772. Who would sign off on the charter?

773. Have the key elements of a coherent Web Customer Support project management strategy been established?

774. Are changes in scope (deliverable commitments) agreed to by all affected groups & individuals?

775. Have all stakeholders been identified?

776. What is the general purpose in defining responsibilities of the already stated affiliated with the Web Customer Support project?

777. Does the system design reflect the requirements?

778. Is an industry recognized mechanized support tool(s) being used for Web Customer Support project scheduling & tracking?

779. Are Web Customer Support project team members committed fulltime?

780. Has a Web Customer Support project Communications Plan been developed?

781. Pareto diagrams, statistical sampling, flow charting or trend analysis used quality monitoring?

782. Has the Web Customer Support project manager been identified?

2.39 Change Management Plan: Web Customer Support

783. What processes are in place to manage knowledge about the Web Customer Support project?

784. How does the principle of senders and receivers make the Web Customer Support project communications effort more complex?

785. What prerequisite knowledge do corresponding groups need?

786. What is going to be done differently?

787. How prevalent is Resistance to Change?

788. What are the needs, priorities and special interests of the audience?

789. Who will be the change levers?

790. Is there a software application relevant to this deliverable?

791. What are the major changes to processes?

792. What new behaviours are required?

793. Where do you want to be?

794. What are the responsibilities assigned to each role?

795. What are you trying to achieve as a result of communication?

796. What risks may occur upfront, during implementation and after implementation?

797. What are the training strategies?

798. Has the training provider been established?

799. When does it make sense to customize?

800. What work practices will be affected?

3.0 Executing Process Group: Web Customer Support

801. When will the Web Customer Support project be done?

802. What are some crucial elements of a good Web Customer Support project plan?

803. What are the main types of goods and services being outsourced?

804. What are deliverables of your Web Customer Support project?

805. Does the case present a realistic scenario?

806. When do you share the scorecard with managers?

807. What are the critical steps involved with strategy mapping?

808. What good practices or successful experiences or transferable examples have been identified?

809. How well did the team follow the chosen processes?

810. Who will provide training?

811. Is the Web Customer Support project performing better or worse than planned?

812. Based on your Web Customer Support project communication management plan, what worked well?

813. Does software appear easy to learn?

814. What are deliverables of your Web Customer Support project?

815. How do you enter durations, link tasks, and view critical path information?

816. Who will be the main sponsor?

817. Will outside resources be needed to help?

3.1 Team Member Status Report: Web Customer Support

818. The problem with Reward & Recognition Programs is that the truly deserving people all too often get left out. How can you make it practical?

819. Are the products of your organizations Web Customer Support projects meeting customers objectives?

820. When a teams productivity and success depend on collaboration and the efficient flow of information, what generally fails them?

821. Is there evidence that staff is taking a more professional approach toward management of your organizations Web Customer Support projects?

822. How much risk is involved?

823. How will resource planning be done?

824. Why is it to be done?

825. Are the attitudes of staff regarding Web Customer Support project work improving?

826. How does this product, good, or service meet the needs of the Web Customer Support project and your organization as a whole?

827. Will the staff do training or is that done by a third

party?

828. What specific interest groups do you have in place?

829. Does the product, good, or service already exist within your organization?

830. Does your organization have the means (staff, money, contract, etc.) to produce or to acquire the product, good, or service?

831. Does every department have to have a Web Customer Support project Manager on staff?

832. What is to be done?

833. Do you have an Enterprise Web Customer Support project Management Office (EPMO)?

834. How it is to be done?

835. Are your organizations Web Customer Support projects more successful over time?

836. How can you make it practical?

3.2 Change Request: Web Customer Support

837. When to submit a change request?

838. Change request coordination ?

839. What needs to be communicated?

840. Customer acceptance plan how will the customer verify the change has been implemented successfully?

841. What type of changes does change control take into account?

842. Should a more thorough impact analysis be conducted?

843. Can static requirements change attributes like the size of the change be used to predict reliability in execution?

844. Who is included in the change control team?

845. Who can suggest changes?

846. How do team members communicate with each other?

847. Will all change requests be unconditionally tracked through this process?

848. Has your address changed?

849. Will this change conflict with other requirements changes (e.g., lead to conflicting operational scenarios)?

850. How fast will change requests be approved?

851. Screen shots or attachments included in a Change Request?

852. How can changes be graded?

853. Have all related configuration items been properly updated?

854. Since there are no change requests in your Web Customer Support project at this point, what must you have before you begin?

855. What can be filed?

3.3 Change Log: Web Customer Support

856. Is the requested change request a result of changes in other Web Customer Support project(s)?

857. Is the change backward compatible without limitations?

858. When was the request approved?

859. Is the submitted change a new change or a modification of a previously approved change?

860. Is the change request open, closed or pending?

861. How does this relate to the standards developed for specific business processes?

862. How does this change affect the timeline of the schedule?

863. Where do changes come from?

864. Do the described changes impact on the integrity or security of the system?

865. How does this change affect scope?

866. When was the request submitted?

867. Is the change request within Web Customer Support project scope?

868. Is this a mandatory replacement?

869. Does the suggested change request represent a desired enhancement to the products functionality?

870. Will the Web Customer Support project fail if the change request is not executed?

871. Who initiated the change request?

3.4 Decision Log: Web Customer Support

872. At what point in time does loss become unacceptable?

873. With whom was the decision shared or considered?

874. How does provision of information, both in terms of content and presentation, influence acceptance of alternative strategies?

875. Who is the decisionmaker?

876. How do you know when you are achieving it?

877. What alternatives/risks were considered?

878. Do strategies and tactics aimed at less than full control reduce the costs of management or simply shift the cost burden?

879. How effective is maintaining the log at facilitating organizational learning?

880. Does anything need to be adjusted?

881. Who will be given a copy of this document and where will it be kept?

882. What is the average size of your matters in an applicable measurement?

883. Decision-making process; how will the team make decisions?

884. What is the line where eDiscovery ends and document review begins?

885. Adversarial environment. is your opponent open to a non-traditional workflow, or will it likely challenge anything you do?

886. What is your overall strategy for quality control / quality assurance procedures?

887. What are the cost implications?

888. How consolidated and comprehensive a story can you tell by capturing currently available incident data in a central location and through a log of key decisions during an incident?

889. Behaviors; what are guidelines that the team has identified that will assist them with getting the most out of team meetings?

890. What was the rationale for the decision?

891. How does the use a Decision Support System influence the strategies/tactics or costs?

3.5 Quality Audit: Web Customer Support

892. How does your organization know that its relationships with the community at large are appropriately effective and constructive?

893. Is your organizations resource allocation system properly aligned with its collection of intentions?

894. How does your organization know that its research funding systems are appropriately effective and constructive in enabling quality research outcomes?

895. How does your organization know that its research planning and management systems are appropriately effective and constructive in enabling quality research outcomes?

896. Is your organizational structure a help or a hindrance to deployment?

897. Are all staff empowered and encouraged to contribute to ongoing improvement efforts?

898. How does your organization know that the range and quality of its social and recreational services and facilities are appropriately effective and constructive in meeting the needs of staff?

899. How does your organization know that the support for its staff is appropriately effective and

constructive?

900. Are training programs documented?

901. How does your organization know that the quality of its supervisors is appropriately effective and constructive?

902. Are the intentions consistent with external obligations (such as applicable laws)?

903. How does your organization know that its Governance system is appropriately effective and constructive?

904. What mechanisms exist for identification of staff development needs?

905. How does your organization know that its systems for providing high quality consultancy services to external parties are appropriately effective and constructive?

906. Does everyone know what they are supposed to be doing, how and why?

907. How does your organization know that it is appropriately effective and constructive in preparing its staff for organizational aspirations?

908. How does your organization know that its processes for managing severance are appropriately effective, constructive and fair?

909. How does your organization know that its information technology system is serving its needs as

effectively and constructively as is appropriate?

910. Statements of intent remain exactly that until they are put into effect. The next step is to deploy the already stated intentions. In other words, do the plans happen in reality?

3.6 Team Directory: Web Customer Support

911. Decisions: is the most suitable form of contract being used?

912. Process decisions: are all start-up, turn over and close out requirements of the contract satisfied?

913. How will the team handle changes?

914. Timing: when do the effects of communication take place?

915. Why is the work necessary?

916. Do purchase specifications and configurations match requirements?

917. Process decisions: which organizational elements and which individuals will be assigned management functions?

918. Process decisions: how well was task order work performed?

919. Process decisions: are there any statutory or regulatory issues relevant to the timely execution of work?

920. When does information need to be distributed?

921. Have you decided when to celebrate the Web

Customer Support projects completion date?

922. Who are the Team Members?

923. What are you going to deliver or accomplish?

924. How will you accomplish and manage the objectives?

925. Where will the product be used and/or delivered or built when appropriate?

926. Days from the time the issue is identified?

927. Who should receive information (all stakeholders)?

928. Is construction on schedule?

3.7 Team Operating Agreement: Web Customer Support

929. How does teaming fit in with overall organizational goals and meet organizational needs?

930. Does your team need access to all documents and information at all times?

931. Do you ensure that all participants know how to use the required technology?

932. What is culture?

933. How will you divide work equitably?

934. Did you prepare participants for the next meeting?

935. Do you post meeting notes and the recording (if used) and notify participants?

936. Are leadership responsibilities shared among team members (versus a single leader)?

937. Do you prevent individuals from dominating the meeting?

938. Do team members need to frequently communicate as a full group to make timely decisions?

939. Resource allocation: how will individual team

members account for time and expenses, and how will this be allocated in the team budget?

940. To whom do you deliver your services?

941. Do you send out the agenda and meeting materials in advance?

942. How will you resolve conflict efficiently and respectfully?

943. What is group supervision?

944. Do you call or email participants to ensure understanding, follow-through and commitment to the meeting outcomes?

945. Do you record meetings for the already stated unable to attend?

946. Are there differences in access to communication and collaboration technology based on team member location?

947. Did you delegate tasks such as taking meeting minutes, presenting a topic and soliciting input?

3.8 Team Performance Assessment: Web Customer Support

948. To what degree are the goals realistic?

949. To what degree are sub-teams possible or necessary?

950. To what degree can team members frequently and easily communicate with one another?

951. When a reviewer complains about method variance, what is the essence of the complaint?

952. To what degree will the team ensure that all members equitably share the work essential to the success of the team?

953. To what degree do team members agree with the goals, relative importance, and the ways in which achievement will be measured?

954. To what degree do team members articulate the teams work approach?

955. To what degree can team members meet frequently enough to accomplish the teams ends?

956. Individual task proficiency and team process behavior: what is important for team functioning?

957. To what degree does the teams purpose contain themes that are particularly meaningful and

memorable?

958. How do you keep key people outside the group informed about its accomplishments?

959. To what degree will new and supplemental skills be introduced as the need is recognized?

960. To what degree does the teams purpose constitute a broader, deeper aspiration than just accomplishing short-term goals?

961. To what degree are the skill areas critical to team performance present?

962. Can team performance be reliably measured in simulator and live exercises using the same assessment tool?

963. How does Web Customer Support project termination impact Web Customer Support project team members?

964. Which situations call for a more extreme type of adaptiveness in which team members actually re-define roles?

965. To what degree do members understand and articulate the same purpose without relying on ambiguous abstractions?

966. What makes opportunities more or less obvious?

3.9 Team Member Performance Assessment: Web Customer Support

967. To what degree are the teams goals and objectives clear, simple, and measurable?

968. For what period of time is a member rated?

969. Are assessment validation activities performed?

970. To what degree do team members feel that the purpose of the team is important, if not exciting?

971. How do you start collaborating?

972. Where can team members go for more detailed information on performance measurement and assessment?

973. Who receives a benchmark visit?

974. New skills/knowledge gained this year?

975. To what degree does the teams approach to its work allow for modification and improvement over time?

976. To what extent did the evaluation influence the instructional path, such as with adaptive testing?

977. How do you currently account for your results in the teams achievement?

978. To what degree do all members feel responsible for all agreed-upon measures?

979. To what degree do members articulate the goals beyond the team membership?

980. Why were corresponding selected?

981. Does the rater (supervisor) have to wait for the interim or final performance assessment review to tell an employee that the employees performance is unsatisfactory?

982. Are there any safeguards to prevent intentional or unintentional rating errors?

983. What is a significant fact or event?

3.10 Issue Log: Web Customer Support

984. Is there an important stakeholder who is actively opposed and will not receive messages?

985. What steps can you take for positive relationships?

986. Who is involved as you identify stakeholders?

987. Why multiple evaluators?

988. Do you have members of your team responsible for certain stakeholders?

989. Do you feel more overwhelmed by stakeholders?

990. Is access to the Issue Log controlled?

991. Which stakeholders can influence others?

992. What help do you and your team need from the stakeholders?

993. Who is the stakeholder?

994. Do you prepare stakeholder engagement plans?

995. Who is the issue assigned to?

996. Are there too many who have an interest in some aspect of your work?

997. Do you often overlook a key stakeholder or stakeholder group?

998. Are stakeholder roles recognized by your organization?

999. Can you think of other people who might have concerns or interests?

1000. How often do you engage with stakeholders?

1001. Why do you manage human resources?

1002. Who are the members of the governing body?

4.0 Monitoring and Controlling Process Group: Web Customer Support

1003. Accuracy: what design will lead to accurate information?

1004. Are the necessary foundations in place to ensure the sustainability of the results of the programme?

1005. Did the Web Customer Support project team have the right skills?

1006. What areas were overlooked on this Web Customer Support project?

1007. How do you monitor progress?

1008. When will the Web Customer Support project be done?

1009. Did it work?

1010. How many more potential communications channels were introduced by the discovery of the new stakeholders?

1011. How well defined and documented were the Web Customer Support project management processes you chose to use?

1012. How is Agile Web Customer Support project

Management done?

1013. Is it what was agreed upon?

1014. How is agile Web Customer Support project management done?

1015. Propriety: who needs to be involved in the evaluation to be ethical?

1016. How can you monitor progress?

1017. Were escalated issues resolved promptly?

1018. Did the Web Customer Support project team have enough people to execute the Web Customer Support project plan?

1019. Is there undesirable impact on staff or resources?

1020. Do the partners have sufficient financial capacity to keep up the benefits produced by the programme?

4.1 Project Performance Report: Web Customer Support

1021. To what degree is the information network consistent with the structure of the formal organization?

1022. To what degree does the information network provide individuals with the information they require?

1023. How is the data used?

1024. To what degree are the demands of the task compatible with and converge with the relationships of the informal organization?

1025. To what degree does the funding match the requirement?

1026. To what degree will the approach capitalize on and enhance the skills of all team members in a manner that takes into consideration other demands on members of the team?

1027. To what degree are the members clear on what they are individually responsible for and what they are jointly responsible for?

1028. To what degree does the informal organization make use of individual resources and meet individual needs?

1029. To what degree do the relationships of the

informal organization motivate taskrelevant behavior and facilitate task completion?

1030. What is the PRS?

1031. What degree are the relative importance and priority of the goals clear to all team members?

1032. How will procurement be coordinated with other Web Customer Support project aspects, such as scheduling and performance reporting?

1033. To what degree is there centralized control of information sharing?

4.2 Variance Analysis: Web Customer Support

1034. Are the requirements for all items of overhead established by rational, traceable processes?

1035. Are there externalities from having some customers, even if they are unprofitable in the short run?

1036. How are variances affected by multiple material and labor categories?

1037. What can be the cause of an increase in costs?

1038. Can process improvements lead to unfavorable variances?

1039. What are the direct labor dollars and/or hours?

1040. What does an unfavorable overhead volume variance mean?

1041. Are there quarterly budgets with quarterly performance comparisons?

1042. Wbs elements contractually specified for reporting of status to your organization (lowest level only)?

1043. Is the entire contract planned in time-phased control accounts to the extent practicable?

1044. What was the cause of the increase in costs?

1045. Are management actions taken to reduce indirect costs when there are significant adverse variances?

1046. Are there knowledgeable Web Customer Support projections of future performance?

1047. Why do variances exist?

1048. Is all contract work included in the CWBS?

1049. Other relevant issues of Variance Analysis -selling price or gross margin?

1050. How does your organization measure performance?

1051. Do the rates and prices remain constant throughout the year?

1052. Is there a logical explanation for any variance?

1053. When, during the last four quarters, did a primary business event occur causing a fluctuation?

4.3 Earned Value Status: Web Customer Support

1054. Earned value can be used in almost any Web Customer Support project situation and in almost any Web Customer Support project environment. it may be used on large Web Customer Support projects, medium sized Web Customer Support projects, tiny Web Customer Support projects (in cut-down form), complex and simple Web Customer Support projects and in any market sector. some people, of course, know all about earned value, they have used it for years - but perhaps not as effectively as they could have?

1055. What is the unit of forecast value?

1056. How much is it going to cost by the finish?

1057. Are you hitting your Web Customer Support projects targets?

1058. How does this compare with other Web Customer Support projects?

1059. Validation is a process of ensuring that the developed system will actually achieve the stakeholders desired outcomes; Are you building the right product? What do you validate?

1060. Where are your problem areas?

1061. If earned value management (EVM) is so good

in determining the true status of a Web Customer Support project and Web Customer Support project its completion, why is it that hardly any one uses it in information systems related Web Customer Support projects?

1062. Verification is a process of ensuring that the developed system satisfies the stakeholders agreements and specifications; Are you building the product right? What do you verify?

1063. When is it going to finish?

1064. Where is evidence-based earned value in your organization reported?

4.4 Risk Audit: Web Customer Support

1065. What are the outcomes you are looking for?

1066. Are staff committed for the duration of the product?

1067. Have all involved been advised of any obligations they have to sponsors?

1068. Is your organization able to present documentary evidence in support of compliance?

1069. How do you compare to other jurisdictions when managing the risk of ....?

1070. Do you have a clear plan for the future that describes what you want to do and how you are going to do it?

1071. Is the technology to be built new to your organization?

1072. Do end-users have realistic expectations?

1073. Do you have a realistic budget and do you present regular financial reports that identify how you are going against that budget?

1074. Extending the consideration on the halo effect, to what extent are auditors able to build skepticism in evidence review?

1075. Does your organization have any policies or

procedures to guide its decision-making (code of conduct for the board, conflict of interest policy, etc.)?

1076. Strategic business risk audit methodologies; are corresponding an attempt to sell other services, and is management becoming the client of the audit rather than the shareholder?

1077. Is a software Web Customer Support project management tool available?

1078. Are requirements fully understood by the team and customers?

1079. Which assets are important?

1080. Should additional substantive testing be conducted because of the risk audit results?

1081. What can be measured?

1082. Are all participants informed of safety issues?

4.5 Contractor Status Report: Web Customer Support

1083. What are the minimum and optimal bandwidth requirements for the proposed solution?

1084. What was the actual budget or estimated cost for your organizations services?

1085. If applicable; describe your standard schedule for new software version releases. Are new software version releases included in the standard maintenance plan?

1086. How is risk transferred?

1087. What was the budget or estimated cost for your organizations services?

1088. How does the proposed individual meet each requirement?

1089. What was the overall budget or estimated cost?

1090. What was the final actual cost?

1091. Who can list a Web Customer Support project as organization experience, your organization or a previous employee of your organization?

1092. What is the average response time for answering a support call?

1093. What process manages the contracts?

1094. Describe how often regular updates are made to the proposed solution. Are corresponding regular updates included in the standard maintenance plan?

1095. How long have you been using the services?

1096. Are there contractual transfer concerns?

4.6 Formal Acceptance: Web Customer Support

1097. What can you do better next time?

1098. Was the sponsor/customer satisfied?

1099. What function(s) does it fill or meet?

1100. Does it do what Web Customer Support project team said it would?

1101. Did the Web Customer Support project manager and team act in a professional and ethical manner?

1102. How well did the team follow the methodology?

1103. Who supplies data?

1104. Does it do what client said it would?

1105. Who would use it?

1106. Was the Web Customer Support project work done on time, within budget, and according to specification?

1107. What features, practices, and processes proved to be strengths or weaknesses?

1108. Have all comments been addressed?

1109. What is the Acceptance Management Process?

1110. Do you buy pre-configured systems or build your own configuration?

1111. Was the Web Customer Support project managed well?

1112. Do you buy-in installation services?

1113. Was the Web Customer Support project goal achieved?

1114. Did the Web Customer Support project achieve its MOV?

1115. Do you perform formal acceptance or burn-in tests?

1116. Was the client satisfied with the Web Customer Support project results?

5.0 Closing Process Group: Web Customer Support

1117. Were the outcomes different from the already stated planned?

1118. Were sponsors and decision makers available when needed outside regularly scheduled meetings?

1119. Measurable - are the targets measurable?

1120. If a risk event occurs, what will you do?

1121. What is an Encumbrance?

1122. Does the close educate others to improve performance?

1123. How will you know you did it?

1124. Did you do what you said you were going to do?

1125. When will the Web Customer Support project be done?

1126. Contingency planning. if a risk event occurs, what will you do?

1127. What is the Web Customer Support project Management Process?

1128. Are there funding or time constraints?

1129. What were the desired outcomes?

1130. How will staff learn how to use the deliverables?

1131. What will you do to minimize the impact should a risk event occur?

1132. Were risks identified and mitigated?

5.1 Procurement Audit: Web Customer Support

1133. Is there time waste during tendering?

1134. Has the award included no items different from the already stated contained in bid specifications?

1135. Is the minutes book kept current?

1136. Are all claims certified by the officer giving rise to the claim (usually the purchasing agent)?

1137. Did the contracting authority offer unrestricted and full electronic access to the contract documents and any supplementary documents (specifying the internet address in the notice)?

1138. Did the contracting authority draw up a comprehensive written report about progress and outcome of the procurement process?

1139. Are all purchase orders reviewed by someone other than the individual preparing the purchase order (reasonableness of order and vendor selection)?

1140. Is there an effective risk management system continuously monitoring procurement risk?

1141. Is there a formal program of inservice training for personnel in the business management function?

1142. Are criteria and sub-criteria set suitable to

identify the tender that offers best value for money?

1143. Is there ineffective internal communication in the procurement function/unit?

1144. Is there a practice that prohibits signing blank purchase orders?

1145. Must the receipt of goods be approved prior to payment?

1146. Are behaviour modification applied to change procurement of goods and services if procurement is not functioning properly?

1147. Has your organization clearly defined the award criteria?

1148. Is the foreseen budget compared with similar Web Customer Support projects or procurements yet realised (historical standards)?

1149. Are there regular reviews and analysis of the performance of the procurement function/unit?

1150. Is there a procedure on requesting bids?

1151. Is sufficient evidence required for all disbursements (except nominal amounts)?

1152. Can changes be made to automatic disbursement programs without proper approval of management?

5.2 Contract Close-Out: Web Customer Support

1153. Was the contract sufficiently clear so as not to result in numerous disputes and misunderstandings?

1154. Parties: Authorized?

1155. Change in knowledge?

1156. Are the signers the authorized officials?

1157. Has each contract been audited to verify acceptance and delivery?

1158. Was the contract type appropriate?

1159. Have all contract records been included in the Web Customer Support project archives?

1160. What happens to the recipient of services?

1161. Why Outsource?

1162. Have all contracts been closed?

1163. What is capture management?

1164. Was the contract complete without requiring numerous changes and revisions?

1165. How does it work?

1166. Change in circumstances?

1167. Have all acceptance criteria been met prior to final payment to contractors?

1168. Parties: who is involved?

1169. How/when used ?

1170. Change in attitude or behavior?

1171. How is the contracting office notified of the automatic contract close-out?

1172. Have all contracts been completed?

5.3 Project or Phase Close-Out: Web Customer Support

1173. What was the preferred delivery mechanism?

1174. Were cost budgets met?

1175. What is the information level of detail required for each stakeholder?

1176. What are the informational communication needs for each stakeholder?

1177. Can the lesson learned be replicated?

1178. Who is responsible for award close-out?

1179. What was learned?

1180. What security considerations needed to be addressed during the procurement life cycle?

1181. If you were the Web Customer Support project sponsor, how would you determine which Web Customer Support project team(s) and/or individuals deserve recognition?

1182. Is the lesson based on actual Web Customer Support project experience rather than on independent research?

1183. How much influence did the stakeholder have over others?

1184. Was the schedule met?

1185. Which changes might a stakeholder be required to make as a result of the Web Customer Support project?

1186. What is a Risk?

1187. Did the delivered product meet the specified requirements and goals of the Web Customer Support project?

1188. Were messages directly related to the release strategy or phases of the Web Customer Support project?

1189. What is in it for you?

5.4 Lessons Learned: Web Customer Support

1190. How well prepared were you to receive Web Customer Support project deliverables?

1191. What worked well/did not work well?

1192. How was the Web Customer Support project controlled?

1193. What are the conceptual limits of the research?

1194. How well is the build process working?

1195. How well did the Web Customer Support project Manager respond to questions or comments related to the Web Customer Support project?

1196. Were the aims and objectives achieved?

1197. How do security constraints impact the case?

1198. How smooth do you feel Integration has been?

1199. To what extent was the evolution of risks communicated?

1200. How objective was the collection of data?

1201. What are the external dependencies?

1202. What Web Customer Support project

circumstances were not anticipated?

1203. Who is responsible for each action?

1204. How actively and meaningfully were stakeholders involved in the Web Customer Support project?

1205. How effective were Web Customer Support project audits?

1206. What rewards do the individuals seek?

1207. What did you put in place to ensure success?

1208. How accurately and timely was the Risk Management Log updated or reviewed?

1209. Did the Web Customer Support project improve the team members reputations, skills, personal development?

Index

278

300